EFFECTIVE SPEAKING

THE TABLES TURNED!

"NOW, JUST ANSWER A FEW QUESTIONS . . ."

EFFECTIVE SPEAKING

A Course in Elocution

by

J. G. MARASH M.A. L.R.A.M. (Eloc.)

With Drawings by

GWENDOLINE PERKINS

If the working class would concentrate on — accent
— equality would be here in no time.

JOHN GALSWORTHY

Second Edition Revised and Enlarged

HARRAP   LONDON

First published in Great Britain 1947
by GEORGE G. HARRAP & CO. LTD
182 High Holborn, London WC1V 7AX

Reprinted: 1949; 1954; 1957; 1960

Second Edition, revised, 1962

Reprinted: 1964; 1967; 1969; 1972; 1974; 1980

ISBN 0 245 55839 X

Printed and bound in Great Britain by
Redwood Burn Limited
Trowbridge & Esher

BY WAY OF EXCUSE

MOST people who write books seem to feel that they need to make excuses for having done so. Hence the introductions, prefaces, forewords, and apologies. One feels particularly the necessity for walking warily in dealing with a subject whose very name is a fruitful source of controversy—is it to be Elocution, Diction, Speech Training, or what?—and whose teachers each seem to have a different method and system which to them is the only right one. However, here are my excuses! May they prove adequate!

My first idea was to help those examination students and others whose customary complaint is: "I can manage my selections and sight reading, but I shall never answer the questions; I can't find so-and-so in any of the text-books." This book is intended to cover all the work up to and including the final examination in Elocution. For that reason various rules and classifications have been dealt with more fully than they would otherwise have been; such rules may be of use to the examination candidate, but may become a grave danger to the performer if he allows them to get the upper hand. But I hope it will do more than that. Surely such an important subject as this—one that is used in every sphere of life—should not be limited to the few; it should be open to all—to the ambitious, however humble; to those who do not wish to feel 'out of it' in society; and above all to those who would become "students of our sweet English tongue" for its own sake.

One who speaks pure, cultured English will always have the advantage in life. The millionaire social climber who drops his aitches is sadly handicapped compared with the impecunious individual with good accent and manner. No political or economic reforms, not even higher education (as we now understand it), will ever completely wipe out class barriers, but good speech and manner will go far towards doing so.

But there are other and wider considerations. We hear so

much about the beauty and 'music' of other languages. Why, I wonder, should we always think the other man's wares better than our own? What could be more beautiful than our own language—the language of Chaucer, Shakespeare, and Milton? Let us live up to our heritage and see that our own beautiful tongue is beautifully spoken.

It is hoped that this little book will kindle the torch. To you now, the duty of passing it on!

J. G. M.

NOTE TO THE SECOND EDITION

To this new edition have been added two chapters: one on Public Speaking, which it is hoped will be of assistance to speech-makers of all ages and kinds, and one on Choral Speech (Speaking Together). This latter has been written with teachers specially in mind, and with the earnest desire that it may help to raise the standard of speech in educational establishments of all types.

J. G. M.

CONTENTS

LESSON I
VOWEL SOUNDS

We must first decide exactly what we mean when we speak of elocution. Elocution, the dictionary says, is the "art of effective speaking." That is to say, it is the art of 'speaking out' correctly and beautifully and with the appropriate use of facial expression and of gesture.

NOT THIS!

NOR YET THIS!

The student's first study, therefore, should be to speak correctly.

Now, correct speech depends primarily upon three things:

    (1) perfectly formed vowel sounds,

    (2) clearly articulated consonants,

    (3) the following of generally accepted rules of pronunciation.

It must be noted here that we make a distinction between speech that is merely correct and speech that is good and artistic. For the latter we should need to add yet another essential, namely, the proper method of breathing, which will be dealt with in Lesson IV.

Let us deal first with the vowel sounds, because upon these speech relies for its

    (a) purity,

    (b) audibility and carrying power,

    (c) to a large extent, beauty or 'flowing' quality.

We will consider these points in a little more detail.

Purity of Speech

If you recall the various local—and other—'accents' you will see that most of the faults lie chiefly in the production of the vowel sounds. This applies equally to the Cockney 'twang,' to the just-as-bad—if not worse—so-called 'Oxford' accent, and to the would-be genteel.

To speak correctly, then, we must have pure vowel sounds.

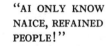

"WANT A PIPER, GUVNER? THE DILY MILE?"

"AI ONLY KNOW NAICE, REFAINED PEOPLE!"

Audibility and Carrying Power

Shepherds on mountain pastures can make their voices carry from hill to hill by prolonging the vowel sounds. An example is to be found in Chapter XXX of Thomas Hardy's *Under the Greenwood Tree*.

Similarly the Muezzin, calling the faithful to prayer from the top of the minaret, makes full use of the vowels.

ALLAH, OU AKBAR. LA
ILLAHA ILLALLAH . . .

If, therefore, you wish to be heard in a large hall or theatre pay attention to your vowel sounds!

Beauty or Flowing Quality

Speech is made up of vowels and consonants. Many consonants are merely noises, so that the beauty of speech depends primarily upon the vowels and the liquid and nasal consonants. The Romance languages are said to be musical, because, in them, prominence is given to the vowel and to the liquid sounds.

So, for beauty in speech, as well as correctness and audibility, you must attend to the vowel sounds.

The question now arises as to whether by vowel sounds we mean a, e, i, o, u?

A HAS SEVEN
OFFSPRING

No! These are the letters, and are merely the symbols representing the sounds. We can regard them as 'fathers of families.' **a**, for instance, has seven offspring: **ǎ** (has); **ah** (last); **ay** (may); **aw** (talk); **ae** (many); **ǒ** (what); **uh** (a̱bout). (◡ indicates short sound.) Altogether the five letter-symbols give us about twenty-two vowel sounds (twenty-six if we count the murmur diphthongs as found in bare, beer, boor, bore).

The following table clearly shows the different classifications into which these vowel sounds can be divided:

Twelve Monophthongs

(Each one sound, which is the same at the end as at the beginning)

Long or Open (can be sustained)		Short or Shut (cannot be sustained)	
ah	(last)	ǎ	(hat)
ur	(her)	ǔh	(the)
aw	(saw)	ǒ	(not)
oo	(cool)	o͝o	(good)
ee	(leaves)	ĭ	(pit)
		ǔ	(much)
		ĕ	(pen)

Four Diphthongs

(Two sounds, one long and one short)

i	(my)	=	a[1]	(French *chat*)	+	ĭ	(pit)
oy	(boy)	=	aw	(saw)	+	ĭ	(pit)
ow	(how)	=	a[1]	(French *chat*)	+	o͝o	(good)
y	(you)	=	e	(me)	+	o͝o	(good)

[1] A sound half-way between ah and ǎ.

Two Vanish Diphthongs

(Two sounds, both short)

ay	(mate)	=	ĕ	(met)	+	ĭ	(pit)
o	(go)	=	o[2]	(French *eau*)	+	o͝o	(good)

[2] For this sound the lips must be rounded and pushed slightly forward.

Four Triphthongs

(Three sounds: long, short, and the neutral vowel uh (the))

ire	(fire)	=	a	(*chat*)	+	ĭ	(pit)	+	u̇h	(the)
oir	(coir)	=	aw	(saw)	+	ĭ	(pit)	+	u̇h	(the)
our	(power)	=	a	(*chat*)	+	o͝o	(good)	+	uh	(the)
ure	(cure)	=	ĭ	(pit)	+	o͞o	(moon)	+	uh	(the)

There will be some difficulty in remembering all these twenty-two sounds; so here are some sentences that will help you. They are in the form of mnemonics—aids to memory.

Long (or open) Monophthongs : He saw her last move.
Short (or shut) Monophthongs : The black pen is not much good.
Diphthongs : My boy, how (are) you?
Vanish Diphthongs : Woe (the) day!
Triphthongs : Cure our (Mr) Doir's ire.

It is of interest and value to notice how vowel sounds are made. The breath coming from the lungs passes through the larynx (the voice box), which we shall discuss more fully in a later lesson. The elastic vocal chords vibrate and sound is made—the 'uh—uh'—of a hesitant speaker—the breath passing out through an uninterrupted passage. The different vowel sounds are made by the relative positions of tongue, lips, and palate.

For practical purposes we divide the vowel sounds into two series or groups :

(*a*) *Lip group*—in which the chief work is done by the lips, and the tongue works a little.

ah, ŏ, **aw**, ō, ŏo, ōo (Karl got Maud's old book too)

(*b*) *Tongue group*—where the lips are used very little and the burden of work falls on the tongue.

ah, **uh**, **er**, ă, ě, **ay**, ĭ, **ee** (Fast gulls turn back, then slay with speed)

These different sounds should be practised, and in order to do so you should take a small mirror and stand in a good light. Hold the chin level and the mirror just before the mouth.

Throughout the exercises the teeth should be practically the same distance apart—*i.e.*, just wide enough to admit the thumb joint—and the tongue tip should be touching the bottom front teeth.

These two points are important.

(*a*) Now carefully repeat the Lip Vowels, throwing the voice forward towards the mirror. The lips are gradually rounded and pushed forward—most forward for ō; most rounded for o͞o. The tongue is flat for **ah**, and is then slightly raised at the back, but the tip is always in contact with the teeth. Test the width of the mouth opening at the end of the exercise.

(*b*) Now repeat the Tongue Vowels. The teeth and tongue position is as for (*a*), but this time the front part of the tongue is raised from the flat position (for **ah**), the tip being still in contact with the teeth. The lips move very little and the student should guard against the tendency to close the teeth and draw the corners of the lips back for the last two sounds.

There are certain pitfalls to be avoided when you are doing these exercises:

1. The jaw must not be stiff.
2. The tongue and lips must be flexible.

Exercises B, C, and D below will help to rectify these errors.

Watch these sounds:

ah (last).	The sound must be at the *front* of the mouth, *not* in the throat.
o͞o (cool).	Do not turn this sound into a diphthong, thus: **oo** + **uh**.
i (my).	Twofold danger. Do not make the sound **ah** + **ee**, and, *whatever you do*, avoid the hideous **ay** + **i** of the 'refayned' folk!
oy (boy).	Do not substitute **i** (by)!
ow (now).	Do not make this sound too broad—not ă (hat) + **oo** (cool).
ay (may).	Be sure that the first sound is ĕ (met).
o (go).	See that the lips are well rounded and that the 2nd sound is short (ŏo).
ire (fire).	Do not turn this into '**fah**' or '**flyer**'
oir (royal).	Do not make this '**ryal.**'
our (power).	Give full value to the ŏo. Do not say 'pạh.'

PRACTICAL EXERCISES

A. *For general practice.*

Do not practise immediately after a meal, or when you feel tired. Relax completely before beginning the exercises—imagine that you are a rag doll.

1. First of all, take up a good standing position. Feet in small V position; knees braced; body held upright—*but not stiffly*; shoulders squared; chin level.

2. Place hands lightly on sides of chest, with elbows pointing sideways. Breathe in through the nose and out through the mouth. Repeat three to six times. Do not take too deep a breath; do not raise the shoulders; keep the abdominal wall firm. Feel expansion at the sides, as well as at the front of chest.

3. Place one hand on abdomen. Draw the abdominal wall in and then release slowly. Repeat rhythmically—*not* in jerks.

4. Breathe in through the nose. Repeat the vowel groups, drawing in abdominal wall as the sound begins and releasing when it ends. (This is known as the *Abdominal Press*). Vowel groups may be repeated with 'm' before each: mah, mŏ, maw, etc.

5. Breathe in through the nose. Hum on one note—humming exercises are excellent for improving tone and resonance.

6. Repeat jingles, or nursery rhymes, for vowel sounds—*e.g.*, *Simple Simon*.

7. Read aloud some fairly simple prose passage, working up to more difficult passages—vary your choice.

When you discover a weakness in your speech *practise daily* until you have corrected it.

B. *To correct stiff jaw.*

Let the jaw drop as far as possible; then close the mouth. Repeat six times.

C. *To make lips flexible.*

1. Practise the lip vowels.
2. Repeat *ah-oo*, *ah-oo* several times.
3. Open the mouth, then draw the lips back, then round the lips,

thus: 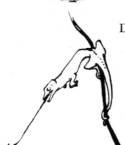   Repeat.

D. *For lazy tongue.* (Do these in private!)

1. Shoot the tongue in and out as far and as hard as possible until it is tired. It will then fall naturally into its right position in the mouth.
2. Practise curling the tip and sides of tongue.

EXERCISES IN THEORY

Answers should be to the point. Do not copy from the lesson but think for yourself! Use diagrams where they make the answer clearer.

1. What is meant by 'Elocution'?
2. Why should the student pay special attention to vowel sounds?
3. On what does correct speech depend?
4. How would you define a vowel?
5. Give two ways of classifying vowel sounds.
6. Give two examples each of (*a*) open monophthongs, (*b*) shut monophthongs, (*c*) diphthongs, (*d*) triphthongs. Say how you would recognize each kind.

7. Classify the vowels in the following words and say carefully how each is formed: cow; low; tyre; mine; rat.
8. Give two or three rules for a good standing position.
9. How would you correct (*a*) a stiff jaw, (*b*) a lazy tongue, (*c*) a stiff upper lip?
10. How would you improve your sight reading?

LESSON II
CONSONANTS

In Lesson I we dealt with the first essential of correct speech—purely formed vowel sounds. We now come to the second essential—clearly articulated consonants.

Consonants are important because upon them speech depends:
- (*a*) for its distinctness,
- (*b*) for its brilliance or verve,
- (*c*) for its firmness.

If you try to give names or unusual words over the telephone you will find that you have little difficulty with the vowels, but

"GI' US THE CORE, BILL!"

"THE' EN'A GON'A BE NO CORE!"

you will soon be reduced to giving "B for Bertie, D for Dolly," because consonants are more easily confused. Much of the speech of those around you sounds slovenly and unfinished because seventy-five per cent. of the speakers rarely pronounce consonants well, especially final consonants. We hear "tha" for tha*t*; "abou" for abou*t*; "an" for an*d*.

A consonant is a sound formed by the complete or partial stoppage of the breath by the organs of articulation—the jaw; the tongue; the teeth; the lips; the hard palate; the soft palate. We speak of the 'articulation' of consonants, because these

18

organs play an important part in their formation. For the formation of the vocal or voiced consonants there is also vibration of the vocal chords.

There are twenty-five consonantal sounds, if we include those which are compounded of other consonants, and they can be classified in several ways. The following table gives all the classifications:

	EXPLOSIVE (cannot be prolonged)		SUSTAINED (can be prolonged)	
	[1]*Aspirate* (unvoiced)	*Vocal* (voiced)	*Aspirate* (unvoiced)	*Vocal* (voiced)
Labials (formed by lips)	p	b	wh	w m (nasal)
Labio-dentals (lips and teeth)			f	v
Lingua-dentals (tongue and teeth)			th (think) s sh	th (though) z zh (azure)
Lingua-palatals (tongue and palate)	t ch	d j		l (liquid) n (nasal) p r
Gutturals (tongue and soft palate)	k	g		ng
Orals (open mouth)			h	y

If you are asked to classify a consonant it should be done in this way:

m is a sustained, vocal consonant, labial and nasal.

t is an explosive, aspirate consonant, and a lingua-palatal.

In order to practise the consonants, take your mirror, as you did for the vowel sounds, and carefully repeat all the sounds in the chart. Remember to say the sound, *not* the alphabet name—'b,' not 'be.'

[1] Aspirate has breath only—no vibration of chords. Vocal has voice added—vibration of chords.

Labials—**p** and **b**. The lips are lightly pressed together, so that the breath passing through them causes a little explosion. **b** has a voice added.

  m: Lips are closed; the breath is forced up through the nose; the sound should be at the *front* of the mouth.

  w: Lips are as for $\overline{oo}$, but with more force.

  wh: The breath passes through rounded lips.

Labio-dentals—**f** and **v**. The bottom lip is lightly held by the top teeth and the breath passes out at the sides of the mouth. **v** has voice added.

Lingua-dentals—**th** and **th** (e). The tongue tip is lightly held between the teeth. **th** (as in *though*) has voice added.

  s and **z**: The sides of the tongue touch the upper teeth and the breath passes down the groove of the tongue (**z** with voice).

Lingua-palatals—**t** and **d**. The tongue tip makes light contact with the hard palate just behind the teeth (**d** has voice); the breath passing through breaks the contact.

  l: There is contact between the front part of the tongue and the hard palate, but in this sound the breath passes out on either side of the tongue.

  n: The position of the tongue is almost the same as for **l**, but the breath passes through the nose.

  r: The tongue tip is curled up against the hard palate, and is made to vibrate by the breath.

Gutturals—**k** and **g**: Here there is contact between the base of the tongue and the soft palate.

  ng: In this sound the breath passes through the nose.

  Orals—**h**: Here the breath passes through the open mouth.

      y: Very like **ee**, but with more force.

Care must be taken with the following points :

  wh: Do not turn this into **w**, but do not exaggerate the aspirate.

  th: Some people (especially young children) substitute **f** for **th**. Care must be taken that the tongue is *between* the teeth.

s: This is a difficult sound for some, who replace it by **th** (lisping). Keep the teeth almost closed.

r: Another difficult sound, something like **w** being the usual substitution. Tongue exercises will help to remove this defect.

m and **n**: See that these sounds have their proper nasal quality. If the nasal passages are blocked, these sounds become **b** and **d**; **ing**—not **in'**, nor **ing**.

h: A bugbear to many! Remember that it is just as bad to put in this sound where it is *not* wanted as to leave it out altogether.

> "Put the heggs in the hoven, hOlive,"
> is worse than
> "'ow can 'arry 'ave the 'eart?"

It is well to remind oneself that any difficulty can be overcome with sufficient determination and patience.

Other instances of careless articulation which must be avoided are:

> 'tha' chew' instead of 'that you'
> 'miss shoo' instead of 'miss you'
> 'an ice'   instead of 'a nice'

Reduplicated consonants (where the same, or similar, consonants follow one another) must also be watched—*e.g.*, mad dog. One must not say 'ma' dog' (one sound), nor yet 'mad-e-dog' (neutral vowel inserted). The student should 'hold' the first sound and carry it on into the next word.

PRACTICAL EXERCISES

It is not, of course, necessary to practise *all* these exercises *every* day. It would be possible to give hundreds of useful exercises, but the student must choose those which will help him most. One may need help with *s*, another with *r*, and so forth.

Exercises which may well be practised daily are marked with **an** asterisk.

*1. Repeat the following sounds (alternate aspirate and vocal consonants and others):

p,b; t,d; ch,j; k,g; f,v; th,th (vocal); s,z; sh,zh; l,n,r; etc.

2. Repeat aspirate consonants: p, t, ch, etc.

3. Repeat vocal consonants: b, d, j, etc.

4. Sound each consonant in turn in front of the vowels: *e.g., pah, pŏ, paw, pō, pŏo, pōo.*

SPECIAL EXERCISES

A. For strengthening soft palate:

1. Breathe in through the nose; out through the mouth.

2. Repeat: *ing-ah*; *ing-ŏ*; *ing-aw*; *ing-ō*; *ing-ŏo*; *ing-ōo*.
   (No 'g,' please.)

B. For *th*:

Place the tongue between the teeth and draw in quickly. Repeat with increasing speed.

C. For *s*:

1. All tongue exercises, as in Exercise D, Lesson I.

2. Practise this sound with these other lingua-palatals:

   t-s-s; *d-s-s*; *l-s-s*; *m-s-s*; and repeat rhythmically.

D. For *r*:

1. Tongue exercises.

2. Put *uh* before *r*:—*uh-*. *uh-r̀*; *uh-r*.

3. *je* (as in 'rouge') *je̒, je, je*—; *je̒, je, je*—; *je̒, je, je*—; *je̒*.

4. Raise tip of tongue a little more and repeat.

5. Raise more still: *re̒, re, re*—; *re̒, re, re*—; *re̒, re, re*—; *re̒*.

The student should make up sentences containing these sounds and practise them carefully (*e.g.,* 'Sister Susie'; 'Peter Piper'). Many examples of such sentences are to be found in books on speech training.

E. Learn by heart these passages from Longfellow's *Hiawatha*:

1. From: "By the shores of Gitchee Gumee . . ."
   to: "Sang the song Nokomis taught him"

   (Hiawatha's Childhood)

2. From: "First he danced a solemn measure . . ."
   to: "Sand hills of the Nagow Wudjoo"

   (Hiawatha's Wedding)

In both cases pay great attention to vowels and consonants.

In the second passage great care must be taken with the consonants, as the rate quickens. *Do not speak more quickly than you are able to articulate clearly.*

EXERCISES IN THEORY

1. What is a consonant and how is it formed?
2. Name the organs of articulation.
3. In what four ways can consonants be classified?
4. What is (*a*) an aspirate, (*b*) a vocal consonant?
5. What is (*a*) an explosive, (*b*) a sustained consonant?
6. Why is it important that consonants should be carefully spoken?
7. Give some common mistakes in the pronunciation of consonants.
8. Classify the consonants in italics in the following words:
   grey *s*ea*s*; *th*in *c*loud*s*; pran*c*in*g Jenny*.
9. What are reduplicated consonants? Give examples.
10. What exercises should be given (*a*) for strengthening the soft palate, (*b*) for lispers, (*c*) for weak *r*?
11. Describe carefully how the following sounds are made:
    l; *m*; *sh*; *ng*; *r*.
12. Make up sentences for the practice of consonants.
    Example: Brave Billy brought Betty back.

LESSON III
PRONUNCIATION

OUR first two lessons have dealt with enunciation, or the way in which words are uttered to obtain the correct sounding of each vowel and consonant. Enunciation is constant and not subject to variation.

Now we come to the third essential of correct speech—pronunciation. This has to do with stress (or accent), with the number of syllables a word contains, with the vowels and consonants which make up the whole word. Pronunciation is liable to change, so that the student must follow the *general* usage of the time. In trying to attain to standard English one can so easily become pedantic, so be sure that you follow the generally accepted pronunciation and never exaggerate even a correct sound! Remember that the Queen's English is a wide belt and includes many slight variations of pronunciation. But all speech to be included in the belt must pass the test that it does not call for remark from the general run of educated people.

Of the many faults in pronunciation the following are among the most common:

(*a*) The placing of stress (or accent) on the wrong syllable: *e.g., exquisite* instead of *èxquisite*; *irrevócable* instead of *irrèvocable*.

(b) Adding syllables or letters: *e.g. admirality* for *admiralty*; *apostle* for *apos'le*; *honour* for *'onour*; *year* for *ear*.

(c) The omission of syllables or letters from words: *e.g., g'ography* for *geography*; *p'raps* for *perhaps*; *goin'*; *dancin'*.

(d) Introduction of wrong vowels or consonants: *e.g., dafferdil* for *daffodil*; *evul* for *evil*; *jew* for *dew*; *nacher* for *nature*; *kitchin* for *kitchen*.

(e) Bridging the hiatus: 'lor of God' for 'law of God.'

Pronunciation can be improved if you will attend to the following suggestions:

(1) Pay attention to the general rules that are given in this lesson.

(2) Listen, whenever possible, to good speakers. In these days of radio and television this is not a difficult matter, but be sure that you imitate only *good* speakers, for their name is not legion!

(3) Read as widely as possible —essays, articles, novels, poetry, the Bible. Read aloud whenever you can. But this in itself is not sufficient. When you meet a new word look up its pronunciation and meaning in a good dictionary. Every student should possess a good dictionary *and should use it*.

I DID HAVE A DICTIONARY SOMEWHERE ... SOME TIME!

Warning

Avoid exaggeration in all things—even in 'correctness'! Never use a long word when a short one will do—'commence' for 'begin' or 'remain' for 'stay.'

Be sure that you use the accepted pronunciation of words, but never an almost unknown or unusual pronunciation, however correct it may be. It will stamp you as a pedant and will draw the attention of the listeners from the subject-matter to the word. This does not mean that you should mispronounce words because the majority of people do so. For instance, do not be tempted to say *despìcable* instead of *dèspicable* because you do not want to appear 'different from others.'

This rule applies also to words and phrases introduced from other languages. Even if you know the correct pronunciation you will only make yourself conspicuous by using it, if the word has become anglicized. At the same time, do not go too far in the opposite direction. A professor of a famous French university refused, on principle, to pronounce 'dancing' and 'pudding' in the English fashion. They had, he declared, become French words, and should therefore be pronounced 'dansinge' and 'poudinge'!

And, lastly, when you *know* how to speak well do not keep your knowledge like your best suit—to be 'put on' for important occasions. Do not lapse into old, careless habits at home or with intimate friends because you do not want to appear to be 'sticking it on'! It is only by constant use that correct speech will become part of yourself so that you are not conscious of it.

Rules of Pronunciation

A. Certain simple rules determine which syllable should be stressed (or accented):

(1) The accent usually comes at the beginning of a word: *e.g.*, pàrdon, dàily, dùtiful.

(2) In words of more than two syllables the main (or primary) accent comes on the first or second syllable and the secondary accent on the fourth or fifth: *e.g.*, hàppily, orìginàlity, àrchaeològical.

(3) Words ending in '-logy,' '-pathy,' '-tion,' '-cracy,' etc., have the accent on the syllable preceding the termination: *e.g.*, biòlogy, osteòpathy, preparàtion, autòcracy.

(4) Pay great attention to these words, which are commonly mispronounced: èxquisite, ìmpious, epìtome (four syllables), irrèvocable, fòrmidable, vèhement, prècedent (noun), precèdent (adjective), consummàte (verb), consùmmate (adjective), perfùme (verb), pèrfume (noun), prìncess, dèspicable, còmparable, ìnteresting, làboratory, àdmirable, indìssoluble, tubèrculòsis, matùre, advèrtisement, hàndkerchief.

B. (1) Great care should be taken not to add letters (or syllables) to words:
'admiralty,' not 'admirality'; 'umbrella,' not 'umberella'; 'Westminster,' not 'Westminister'; 'priority,' not 'prioritry'; 'subtract,' not 'substract.'

"HE ANSWERED THE ADVERTISEMENT AND GOT A JOB IN THE ADMIRALITY"

(2) Silent letters must not be sounded:
epistle, apostle—*t* not sounded; subtle—*b* not sounded.
chasm, chaos—*k*, not *ch*.
heir, honour, hour—*h* not sounded.
pneumonia, pneumatic—*p* not sounded.
C. Letters or syllables must not be omitted:
'perambulator,' not 'p'rambulator'
'perhaps,' not 'p'haps'

'eleven,' not ''leven'
'violet,' not 'vi'let'
'geography,' not 'g'ography'
'home,' not ''ome'
'hoping,' not ''oping'
'history,' not 'histry'

D. One sound should not be substituted for another:

'agony,' not 'agerny'
'daffodil,' not 'dafferdil' ⎱ but do not
'police,' not 'perlice' ⎰ stress the 'o'!
'nothing,' not 'nothink'
'educate,' not 'ejucate'
'dew,' not 'jew'
'February,' not 'Febuary'
'ordnance,' not 'audience'
'picture,' not 'pitcher'
'just,' not 'jist'

E. A careful watch should be kept for words in which pronunciation differs from spelling, such as:

plover(pluvver); inveigh(invay); psychology(sikology); pseudo (sudo); allege (alledj); diphtheria (diftheria); schizocarp (skizokarp); schism (sizm); proboscis (pro-bosis); phlegm (flem).

F. Bridging the hiatus—a very common and bad fault—must be avoided.

The hiatus is the break which comes between two vowel sounds, either in the same word (*e.g.*, co-operation) or in two succeeding words (*e.g.*, china apple). The hiatus is bridged when an *r* or a *w* is inserted between the two vowels (*e.g.*, 'co-w-opera-tion,' 'too-w-awful'; 'the idea-r- of it'). As we have said, this is a serious fault; yet even public speakers are guilty of making it. Therefore watch it carefully. Enunciate the vowels clearly, but do not make the hiatus too noticeable.

It is interesting to note that the hiatus was not accepted in classical French because it destroyed the flow of the verse, and it is avoided even in common speech either by pronouncing the preceding consonant (ils son*t* allés) or by inserting a *t* (y-a-t-il?).

The foregoing are the chief rules of pronunciation. But it must always be borne in mind that nothing can take the place of constant practice in speaking and reading aloud. The student should remember, too, that the dictionary must be in constant use.

EXERCISES

1. State briefly the difference between enunciation and pronunciation.
2. Give three examples of bad enunciation and three of bad pronunciation.
3. What simple rules may be given for the position of the accented syllable?
4. Collect words ending in *-acal*, *-logy*, *-ferous*, and *-tion*, and mark the accent. Check these afterwards by your dictionary.
5. Mark the accented syllables in the following words (using a lighter dash to mark the secondary accent):
   interesting, princess, anthology, indissoluble, perfume, rebel (noun), desert (verb), invalid (adjective), irrevocable, encyclopedia.
6. (The last syllable is called the 'ultimate' syllable; the last but one is the 'penultimate'; the last but two is the 'antipenultimate.')
   Give two words which have the accent on the penultimate syllable (*e.g.*, devouring) and two which have the accent on the anti-penultimate (*e.g.*, inadvertently).
7. "The keynote of good breeding is simplicity." Discuss this statement with special reference to speech.

LESSON IV
BREATH-CONTROL

WE have dealt with the fundamentals of correct speech, and if the preceding lessons have been assimilated the student should now be able to cope with ordinary conversations and the encounters of everyday life without feeling self-conscious and without that awful conviction that he will 'open his mouth and put his foot in it.'

If, however, he is not content with having achieved this, but wishes to train himself for public speaking, even though it be only reading aloud to the family circle—if such an excellent practice still survives!—something more is required than these fundamentals of which we have already spoken.

The first essential for correct public speaking is breath-control. This depends on the right method of breathing, for it must be remembered that there is more than one way of breathing.

To begin with, there is the breathing of life (or breathing of repose) and the breathing for speech or action. The former is involuntary, and goes on without our thinking about it—even when we are asleep. But breathing for speech or action, in the early stages at least, needs considerable thought and practice.

Before we consider the various methods of breathing it is well that we should know something of the respiratory mechanism—the organs for breathing and how they work.

The diagram on p. 31 shows us the bony framework of the chest (the thorax) and the big muscle (the diaphragm) which forms the floor of the chest. This framework is composed of twelve pairs of ribs. Two pairs—the floating ribs—cannot be seen in the diagram, because they do not join the sternum—(breast bone) in front. The ribs protect the heart and lungs. Most people think that the entire work of respiration, or breathing, is done by the lungs alone. In one way this is true, but it is well to remember that the lungs expand only as much as the ribs and diaphragm allow.

The space within the chest wall is increased when the ribs, rotating on joints situated on the vertebrae, are brought from a slanting into a horizontal position. Moreover, although the ribs themselves are made of bone, they are attached to the breast

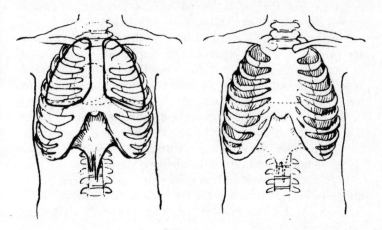

bone and backbone by cartilages (costal cartilages) which can be stretched.

Between each pair of ribs there are two sets of muscles known as the internal and external intercostal muscles. By contracting and expanding, these muscles help to raise and lower the ribs. We may note, in passing, that other muscles — such as the levatores costarum — which are attached to the vertebrae and the ribs below them, play their part in raising and lowering the ribs.

The diaphragm — the big, umbrella-like muscle which forms the ceiling of the abdomen — can be depressed as much as $3\frac{1}{2}$ inches or as little as half an inch in breathing.

The lungs — two spongy elastic bags, composed of air tubes and cells, in appearance rather like a tree turned upside down, are attached to the windpipe (trachea) by the bronchial tubes.

At the top of the windpipe is the voice box (the larynx), of which more will be said later in the book.

As the ribs move upward and outward and the diaphragm flattens, air is drawn into the lungs, which expand until the whole chest space is filled. This is 'breathing in,' known as inspiration, or inhalation.

Then the chest wall and diaphragm return to their normal positions and the air is forced out of the lungs. This is 'breathing out,' called expiration, or exhalation.

Breathing can be controlled because the intercostal muscles are voluntary in their action. The diaphragm—though itself an involuntary muscle—can be controlled through the transverse abdominal muscles, by means of which the abdominal wall can be moved in and out. If the abdominal wall is drawn in, the organs inside press upon the diaphragm, which is forced upward. If, on the other hand, the abdominal muscles are allowed to relax, the diaphragm flattens, presses on the organs of the abdomen, and forces the abdominal wall out.

If this mechanism is borne in mind there should be no difficulty in understanding the methods of respiration.

There are three methods of breathing for speech. They are:

(a) The upper chest or clavicular (clavicle—shoulder blade) method.

(b) The lower chest or abdominal method.

(c) The whole chest or intercostal diaphragmatic method.

We will consider them in order, taking the least desirable method first:

(a) *Upper-chest breathing.* By this method the upper part of the lungs is filled with air. The diaphragm is depressed only half an inch and an attempt is made to move the fixed upper ribs; as a result the shoulders are forced up. Hence the term 'clavicular method.' The effect of this is to cause the chest and throat to become stiff and strained; there is no breath control or bellows power; the voice is harsh. If constantly practised this method will produce throat and chest troubles. It should, therefore, never be used except, perhaps, for dramatic work where some violent, hysterical emotion, such as gasping or sobbing, is required.

UPPER-CHEST BREATHING

Chin drawn in; harsh voice; protruding, stiff chest; shoulders drawn back; hollow back; weight forward on toes.

LOWER-CHEST BREATHING

Chin poked out; breathy voice; undeveloped chest; protruding abdomen; shoulders forward; back rounded; weight on heels.

(b) *Lower-chest breathing*. Here the lungs expand chiefly from top to bottom. The chest wall moves very little, while the diaphragm descends $3\frac{1}{2}$ inches and the abdominal wall is forced out. This method gives very little control or bellows power, and the voice is breathy. The chest is insufficiently developed and the abdomen protrudes.

(c) *Whole-chest breathing*. This is the best method and the one which should be used by all speakers. As its name suggests, the whole chest is used, but attention is concentrated on the centre part (about the sixth and seventh ribs). It is possible to obtain the greatest expansion at this point as the ribs and their cartilages are longer and more curved. The ribs are drawn upward and outward by the action of the intercostal muscles; the abdominal wall is firm (neither protruding nor retracted) so that the diaphragm flattens $1\frac{1}{2}$ inches only. Thus the chest expands in *all* directions.

WHOLE-CHEST BREATHING
  Chin normal; chest healthy; shoulders square; back normal; good balance.

Expiration is controlled by the contraction of the intercostal muscles and by the 'Abdominal Press'—the gradual drawing in of the abdominal wall by the transverse abdominal muscles.

Whole-chest breathing results in perfect control and bellows power. The voice tone is good, and physical development is normal.

PRACTICAL EXERCISES

It will now be possible for the student to practise again, with more understanding, the first four exercises in Lesson I.

There are, of course, innumerable breathing exercises which may be used with advantage. Here are a few that may prove helpful.

1. Adopt a normal standing (or lying) position. Breathe in a medium breath through the nose. Breathe out through the mouth. Repeat.

   Remember that you will do harm rather than good by breathing too deeply. It is a mistake to think that a speaker must always take deep breaths. Short and medium ones are also wanted. In speaking, take in just as much breath as you will need for the phrase you are about to speak. It is a good idea for beginners to practise breathing exercises while lying on the floor, for the body is then in a good position.

2. (for breath control). Breathe in through the nose. Breathe out to a prolonged hum, or to numbers if preferred; but humming, if well done, serves more than one purpose.
Do not continue the sound until you have to gasp for breath. This is harmful.

3. Breathe in for three counts; hold breath for three counts; breathe out for three counts. Repeat, increasing the counts.

4. Practise speaking medium and-long phrases from prose or verse, with one breath. (Turner's *Ecstasy*; Bridges' *Nightingales*; etc.)

Remember, too, that all physical exercises and games are breathing exercises of the best kind, because they are natural.

EXERCISES IN THEORY

1. What is (*a*) inspiration, (*b*) exhalation?
2. What is the difference between the breathing of repose and the breathing for speech?
3. Name the various methods of breathing.
4. Describe in detail the best method of breathing.
5. Give reasons why the other methods should be avoided.
6. Describe, with a diagram if possible: (*a*) the lungs, (*b*) the diaphragm, (*c*) the intercostal muscles.
7. What do you understand by the term 'abdominal press'?
8. What is an 'involuntary' muscle? Name one and also one 'voluntary' muscle.
9. How would you make your breath last for a very long phrase?
10. Can your standing position affect your breathing?
11. How can your method of breathing affect your body and health?

VOICE

We have studied breathing and breath-control, but you may well ask what this has to do with speech. It is an important point, and here again, in order to understand the answer fully, we must learn something of the mechanism of the vocal organs.

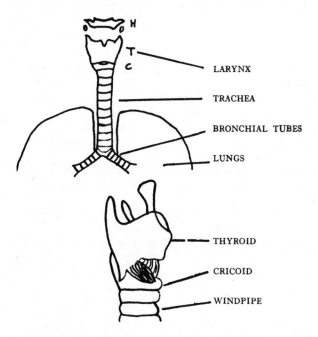

LARYNX

TRACHEA

BRONCHIAL TUBES

LUNGS

THYROID

CRICOID

WINDPIPE

From the lungs two tubes known as the bronchial tubes lead up to the windpipe, or trachea. The trachea is composed of incomplete rings of cartilage, and at the top of it is the larynx (the voice box), also formed of cartilages.

The bottom cartilage, which is shaped like a signet ring, is the cricoid cartilage; into this are fitted the thyroid cartilages, shaped like a screen, which protect the two delicate vocal chords. You can feel the joined part of this screen if you touch your Adam's apple.

The vocal chords are made of elastic tissue, and one end of each is attached to the joint of the thyroid 'screen'; the other ends are connected to two pitcher-shaped cartilages (the arytenoid cartilages), which can rotate. Certain muscles attached to these cartilages can approximate or separate the chords. Others, by tilting the cricoid cartilage, can stretch the chords and make them taut.

When the vocal chords are stretched, the breath passing out from the lungs makes the chords vibrate. This causes the column of air to vibrate, and so sound is produced.

Whether the quality of the sound produced by the vocal chords is toneless or toneful will depend not only on the way in which the breath is brought to bear on the vocal chords but also to a very large extent upon the matter of resonance. A resonant voice, like a correctly tightened drum, has a resounding quality, for it makes full use of the resonators. These are the parts of the vocal mechanism that amplify the sound produced in the larnyx. They are all hollow chambers, and consist of: the chest—to a slight degree; the pockets of the larynx, situated just above the vocal chords; the pharynx—the hollow tube at the back of the mouth and nose, connecting the larynx with the nasal cavities; the mouth; the nose; and the sinuses.

The sinuses are very important. They are the cavities above the eyes and at the back of the nose (frontal and sphenoidal sinuses). If we gave more thought to these important cavities not only would tone be improved, but much discomfort and ill-health would be avoided. If they are filled with mucus and stagnant air they inevitably become the breeding-ground for disease.
Exercises such as those given at the end of this lesson, should be practised daily, so that the sinuses are kept clear and the air

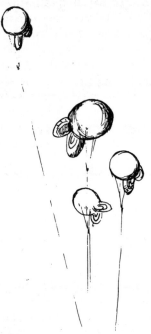

in them renewed. Where this is done regularly, there will be fewer head colds and less catarrh and sinus trouble.

Tone should be buoyant, not 'flat.' You must try to keep it up, like a balloon held up by a puff of wind. This will help to give your speech the 'full' quality that it needs.

Voice also requires 'forward placing,' or it will become throaty and muffled. It is very easy to produce sounds (like 'ah' or a hum) in the back of the mouth and throat. You can tell whether a 'hum' is forward placed by plucking the lips. Keep the tongue forward and, when practising, be 'face conscious,' letting the sound float out lightly to your mirror.

PRACTICAL EXERCISES

A. *For audible and flowing speech.*

   1. Exercises on the vowel sounds—especially long vowels:
         mah, mŏ, maw; mō, mŏo, mōō.
         ahm, ŏm, awm; ōm, ŏom, ōōm.

   2. Repeat the exercises with tongue vowels.

   3. Take a few lines of verse containing long vowels and diphthongs. Say them slowly, prolonging the vowel sounds. Quicken the pace, but never allow your speech to become jerky.

         e.g., Slow-ly si-lently now the moo-n
            Walks the night in her silver shoo-n.

B. *For distinct, firm speech.*

   1. Practise the exercises given for consonants in Lesson II.

2. Repeat short vowels followed by explosive consonants:
   ăt, ĕt, ĭt, ŏt, ŭt, ŏot.
   ăp, ĕp, ĭp, ŏp, ŭp, ŏop.
3. As Exercise B1, but with consonants also before the vowels:
   tăt, tĕt, tĭt, tŏt, tŭt, tŏot.

C. *For forward placing* (tongue tip touching teeth).

1. Repeat six times: *i* (fit); *e* (wet); *ay* (may).
2. Repeat with labial consonants:
   bĭ, bĕ, bay
   mĭ, mĕ, may
3. Repeat C2, adding ah:
   bĭ, bĕ, bay; bah-ah
4. Repeat *ah-ō*; *ah-ō*. Be sure that the sounds are in front of the mouth.

D. *For resonance—freedom and fullness of speech.*

Humming is excellent, providing that the hum is well forward, and can be practised at any time—if it is done discreetly—in the street, in your bath, in bed. Practise as much as you can.

1. Hum on a medium note (feel the vibration of the lips).
2. Allow the voice to slide up and down (not too far) thus /\/\/\
   to: *m, n*, and *ng* (nasal consonants).
3. Hold little humming talks with yourself or with a friend.
4. Hum very softly in a half-voice:
   Repeat to ōo (and other vowel sounds), but return frequently to hum.

This exercise will develop 'tone' and 'restraint.'

5. Repeat passages containing nasal consonants,

   e.g., I murmur under moon and stars.

   Thy sweet child sleep, the filmy-eyed,
   Murmured like a noontide bee,
   'Shall I nestle at thy side?' . . .

EXERCISES IN THEORY

1. How is breath turned into voice?
2. Describe, with diagram, the mechanism of the vocal organs.
3. What is meant by resonance?
4. Name the resonators in order of importance.
5. What exercises would you use to increase resonance?
6. What is meant by 'forward placing'? Why is it important?
7. How would you define tone? On what does good tone depend?
8. Name five qualities of a good speaking voice.
9. State briefly what is the work of: (*a*) the trachea, (*b*) the vocal chords, (*c*) the thyroid cartilages, (*d*) the pharynx.
10. Give exercises for correcting 'jerky' speech.

MODULATION (1): PITCH AND PACE

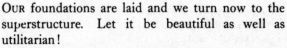

Our foundations are laid and we turn now to the superstructure. Let it be beautiful as well as utilitarian!

However correct speech may be, however good the tone, there can be no true beauty in it without contrast. Nature and life are made up of contrasts, and our appreciation is in proportion to the degree of the contrast. We fully appreciate the shade only when we have been exposed to the burning heat and blinding light of the sun; rain is welcome after prolonged drought; joy is most valued after intense sorrow.

Similarly speech needs change to save it from monotony. Hence the importance of modulation.

Modulation

The text-books tell us that "modulation is the correct and artistic use of pitch, pace, pause, inflexion, tone amount, and tone quality." Now, you should beware of trotting out text-book definitions. To do so shows lack of imagination, if not of intelligence, but such definitions are often useful to keep at the back of one's mind for quick reference.

Pitch and pace (or rate) have much in common, so we will consider them first.

Pitch

"Pitch," says the text-book, "is the key in which anything is sung or spoken." Simply put, therefore, it is a question of

how high or low the voice is. In music and singing there are
many keys or 'pitches,' but in speech we may say that there are
three main pitches—high, medium, and low.

Let us first take *Medium Pitch*, since this is the one we
employ most frequently.   We use it for ordinary conversation
for description, and for meditation or reflexion.

Conversation

> I saw Mrs Brown
> and she said . . .

Description

> On one side lay the Ocean and on one
> Lay a great water, and the moon was full.
>
> > TENNYSON

Reflexion

> For oft, when on my couch I lie
> In vacant or in pensive mood,
> They flash upon that inward eye
> Which is the bliss of solitude;
>
> > WORDSWORTH

High Pitch is the pitch of violent or hysterical emotion. It
is used for anger, surprise, joy, fear, and excitement of any
kind.

> "Off with their heads," shrieked the Queen.
> > LEWIS CARROLL, *Alice in Wonderland*

> Hell is empty and all the devils are here!
> > *The Tempest*

> "Stop, stop, John Gilpin. Here's the house,"
> They all at once did cry.
> > WILLIAM COWPER, *John Gilpin*

Low Pitch is used for any sad or solemn utterance, though it can also be employed for intense anger and fear.

When I consider how my light is spent
Ere half my days in this dark world and wide.
      JOHN MILTON, *On his Blindness*

    One more Unfortunate,
    Weary of breath,
    Rashly importunate,
    Gone to her death!
      THOMAS HOOD, *The Bridge of Sighs*

As we have already said, we change the pitch of our voices in order to avoid monotony, but we must be guided by truth and meaning and not merely by rules. There are several reasons for changing pitch:

(*a*) When the passage spoken indicates a change of feeling, as, for example, from surprise to sorrow.

(*b*) When there is a change of subject.

(*c*) To indicate different characters in dramatic selections—a higher pitch would be used for a woman than for a man.

(*d*) In speaking a parenthesis a lower pitch and quicker pace should be used. (A parenthesis is a phrase added to a sentence, which would, however, be grammatically complete without it.)

    Example:
      By whose aid—weak masters though ye be—
      I have bedimmed the noontide sun.
                 The Tempest

Pace

Pace is the rate at which we speak, and, as in the case of pitch, there are really three paces—quick, medium, and slow.

Medium Pace is the most frequently used, for it is the pace of ordinary conversation, description, and reflexion.

On either side the river lie
Long fields of barley and of rye.
                    TENNYSON, *The Lady of Shalott*

"In that direction," said the cat . . . , "lives a March hare."
                    LEWIS CARROLL, *Alice in Wonderland*

Quick Pace is required for the expression of strong emotion
or for any passage describing rapid movement:

Then more swiftly and still swifter,
Whirling, spinning round in circles.
                    LONGFELLOW, *Hiawatha*

I galloped, Dirk galloped, we galloped all three.
                    BROWNING

The sport was at its height, the sliding was at the quickest, the
laughter was at the loudest, when a sharp, smart crack was
heard.

A warning is necessary here. Some people can articulate
more quickly than others. But the ability to speak rapidly can
be acquired by careful practice. Yet good articulation
should never be sacrificed to speed. There is a general
tendency, especially in sight reading, to speak too
quickly, and this usually results in careless, slipshod
speech. Remember, however, that it is just as bad to
drawl, so try to attain a happy medium.

Slow Pace is used for passages expressive of sorrow,
dignity or solemn reflexion:

Oh God of battles! steel my soldiers' hearts;
. . . take from them now
The sense of reckoning.

                    King Henry V

Avenge, O Lord, thy slaughtered saints, whose bones
  Lie scattered on the Alpine mountains cold.

                    MILTON

Would God I had died for thee, O Absalom, my son, my son.
                    2 Samuel xviii, 33

We should note here that the short vowel sounds (like short notes in music) give us light, rapid phrases, whereas the long vowels and diphthongs (like the long notes) slow down the pace and add dignity to speech.

> Snow drifting gently, fine and white,
> Out of the endless Polar night,
> Falling and falling evermore
> Upon that far untravelled shore. . . .
>
> The carter cracked a sudden whip.
> W. W. GIBSON, *The Ice-cart*

> Ah, Moon of my Delight that know'st no wane.
> EDWARD FITZGERALD, *The Rubá'iyát of Omar Khayyám*

In the same way trisyllabic feet in verse increase the rate, whereas the disyllabic foot is usually slower and more dignified.

> The Assyrian came down like a wolf on the fold.
> BYRON

> As we rush, as we rush in the train,
> The trees and the houses go wheeling back.
> J. THOMSON

PRACTICAL EXERCISES

1. Dramatic work gives plenty of scope for practice in change of pitch. Choose scenes (simple at first, and preferably with only two characters to begin with) and, reading them aloud, concentrate on indicating change of character.
2. Read from an anthology of poems or adventure stories, varying your choice as much as possible.
3. For practice in change of rate read aloud "The Dance of Pau-puk-keewis" (*Hiawatha's Wedding-feast*) and *The Ice-cart* (W. W. Gibson).
4. Read the passages given in this lesson.
   (If you find difficulty in speaking quickly, give extra time to the practice of the short vowels followed by consonants—ăt, ĕt, ĭt, ŏt, ŭt, ŏŏt.

EXERCISES IN THEORY

1. Why must we have change of pitch and pace in elocution?
2. What is modulation?
3. What is pitch, how many pitches are there, and for what is each used?
4. If you were performing for a blind audience how would you show the difference between (a) a man and a woman, (b) an old man and a young man, (c) a giant and a fairy?
5. How would you show the difference between (a) each of the Three Bears, (b) Jack and the Giant, (c) Winnie the Pooh and Owl, (d) Cæsar and Portia, (e) Viola and Olivia, (f) Falstaff and Prince Hal?
6. Give three examples each of passages which need (a) a quick delivery, (b) slow delivery, (c) medium delivery.

MODULATION (2): INFLEXION, TONE QUALITY, AND TONE AMOUNT

INFLEXION must not be confused with pitch. Just as we can have different notes composing a tune in any key of music, so we can have different inflexions in any pitch in speech. Inflexion is the tune in speech, the upward and downward glide of the voice on any syllable, word, or phrase.

There are six inflexions—simple rising ╱ ; simple falling ╲ ; circumflex rising ╲╱ ; circumflex falling ╱╲ ; compound rising ╱╲╱ ; compound falling ╲╱╲ .

You will ask how and when these different inflexions are to be used. One hesitates to give rules for inflexion, because, by following rules, it is so easy for one's work to become forced and unnatural. Yet, though rules cannot take the place of common sense and feeling, it is possible to find some guidance for the correct type of inflexion for different expressions.

Simple Rising Inflexion is used for prayer, pleading, unfinished statements, and questions that can be answered by 'yes' or 'no.'

Simple Falling Inflexion occurs in commands, finished statements, and questions that cannot be answered by 'yes' or 'no.'

Circumflex Inflexions express doubt, hesitation, and also an antithesis or contrast. "Speech is silver; silence is golden."

Compound Inflexions are used to express irony or intense doubt. "Brutus is an honourable man" (suggesting that he is not).

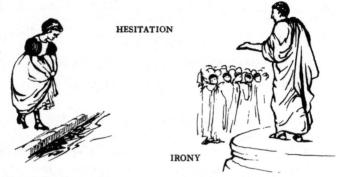

HESITATION

IRONY

The following will, perhaps, best illustrate these different uses:

		Yés?	(What do you want?)
Do you like him?		Yès	(Definite answer—I do.)
,,	,,	Yĕs	(Expressing doubt—I do, but . . .)
,,	,,	Yês	(I've thought it over, and I do on the whole.)
,,	,,	Ỹes	(Greater doubt—I'm not at all sure about it.)
,,	,,	Yȇs	(How could it be otherwise? (irony);—but I don't really)

The student must be warned to avoid over-inflexion—the companion of 'mouthing' and over-acting, and worse than lack of inflexion!

Do not use a falling inflexion at the end of every phrase; save it for the end of the sentence or when the sense is complete. It is, of course, just as bad to overdo the rising inflexion, but it is a much less common fault.

But above all—take the advice of one who has suffered—do not become 'inflexion-ridden.' If you are constantly thinking, 'Now this should have a rising inflexion; I can't get it, but I must practise for hours until I do,' you will destroy your work, which will become artificial and forced. Remember that correct technique can never compensate for the 'living' and individual character of your work.

This is bad:

> When icicles hang by the wàll,
> And Dick the shepherd blows his nàil
> And Tom bears logs into the hàll,
> And milk comes frozen home in pàil . . .

and so also is this:

And thére he saw the sínger, lying upon beaŕskins and fragrant boughs.

When you feel that you have gained experience you must let your own æsthetic sense tell you what kind of inflexion to use. It may not always be technically correct, but it will, at least, be convincing.

Now let us consider Tone Quality and Tone Amount.

Tone Quality: This is the degree of intensity in the voice which causes it to be harsh and hard, or gentle, soft, and mild.

An example will best illustrate the difference in tone quality. Take these two stanzas from James Elroy Flecker's *To a Poet a Thousand Years Hence*:

> I care not if you bridge the seas,
>   Or ride secure the cruel sky,
> Or build consummate palaces
>   Of metal or of masonry.
>
> But have you wine and music still,
>   And statues and a bright-eyed love,
> And foolish thoughts of good and ill,
>   And prayers to them who sit above?

In the first stanza the voice would be hard and cold (even harsh and unsympathetic), while in the second the tone would change until it was soft, appealing, expressive of all longing.

A sonnet—such as D. G. Rossetti's *Without Her*—requires intensity with restraint. The intensity is gradually increased up to the line,

> What of the heart without her?

but the tone never becomes loud—it must be restrained throughout.

Tone Quantity has to do with the degree of sound—the loudness or softness of the voice. Here, as in pitch and pace, there are three degrees—loud, medium, and soft, and once more their use will depend on the sense of the passage.

Medium—for ordinary speech and for description :

> A thing of beauty is a joy for ever.

Loud (combined with high pitch) :

> Must I lie still for ever at his side
> Because you will not rouse yourself ?

Soft (combined with low pitch) :

> Who speaks ? O vanished dew !
> O summer sweetness gone !

It is necessary to offer here one more word of advice. In order to give full value to these contrasts of tone and pitch care must be taken not to use them indiscriminately. The student must remember to 'use all gently' and to be as natural as possible, though 'artistically' natural !

STRONG EMOTION   ORDINARY SPEECH   SAD, SOLEMN

The following table will be found a useful guide:

	Inflexion	Pitch	Pace	Tone quantity	Tone quality[1]
Strong emotion (joy, fear, anger, etc.)	Increased	High	Quick (or quicker)	Loud	Hard[1]
Ordinary Speech (description, reflexion)	Normal	Medium	Medium	Medium	Normal
Sad, Solemn (dignified utterance)	Diminished	Low	Slow (or slower)	Soft[1]	Mild[1]

[1] Note that there are exceptions here. Joy and excitement, for example, though strong feelings, do not need a harsh tone, nor do dignified or solemn utterances require a mild and soft tone.

PRACTICAL EXERCISES

1. Practise the inflexion exercises given in the lesson.
2. Find and read, or learn by heart, passages requiring: (*a*) loud tone, (*b*) medium tone, (*c*) soft tone.
3. Take various passages expressive of deep emotions and speak them in a whisper or half-voice. Remember that you must 'feel' the emotion before you can restrain it! You only feel the power when you rein in a galloping horse—not an 'ambling pad.'

EXERCISES IN THEORY

1. What do you understand by inflexion?
2. How many inflexions do you use? What are they?
3. Would you make any distinction between inflexion and pitch?
4. Write out sentences to illustrate the six main inflexions. Mark them clearly (either /\ or ⁀).
5. Notice what happens in Prospero's speech beginning :

> Ye elves of hills, brooks, standing lakes and groves.
> *The Tempest*, Act V, Scene I

6. Distinguish between tone amount and tone quality.
7. "The student should use extremes of any kind in moderation." Discuss this.
8. "The old actors used often to over-inflect; many modern actors go to the other extreme." How would you help a student to strike the happy medium?

MODULATION (3): PAUSE AND PHRASING

To know how to make effective use of pause is one of the most important lessons for the speaker. Musicians realize the value of the rest or silent bar, and the ancient Hebrew poets understood its importance in verse and made use of it. The 'selah' of the psalms was an indication to the singers to pause; while Isaiah's beautiful Song of the Vineyard has a blank measure (or pause of emotion) to express great sadness. Yet many elocutionists have not learnt the value of the pause. Indeed, most students', especially beginners', main object seems to be to get through a selection with the greatest possible speed and with as few stops—even for breath—as possible. This is especially true of sight reading; to be able to read at a great speed, even if one reads accurately, is not good sight reading.

You must make more use of pause in all phases of your work. An unexpected pause will rouse a dozing audience more quickly than anything else, even though it be only to make them wonder whether you have forgotten your words! But the device must be used with discretion or it will lose its value.

There are six types of pause. Some are to be found only in verse; others in both prose and verse:

Verse Pauses

1. *Cæsural Pause*: This is a short pause in a line of poetry to make the sense clear and to avoid monotony. In English verse there may be one or more of such pauses according to the length of the line. In classical French verse the cæsura divided the Alexandrine into two equal parts:

> Faut-il qu'un si grand cœur // montre
> tant de faiblesse;

but in English verse the cæsura is found in a variety of places
in different lines:

> Look! // in this place ran Cassius' dagger through.
> > *Julius Cæsar*

> I fly thee, // for I would not injure thee.
> > *As You Like It*

> O teach me to see Death // and not to fear.
> > HENRY KING

> Invert
> What best is boded me to mischief! // I
> . . . Do love, // prize, // honour you.
> > *The Tempest*

2. *End-of-the-line pause :* This is normally indicated by the
punctuation:

> Shall I compare thee to a summer's day? //
> Thou art more lovely and more temperate: //
> Rough winds do shake the darling buds of May, //
> And summer's lease hath all too short a date: //
> > WILLIAM SHAKESPEARE

3. *The Suspensory Pause:* This is found at the end of an
enjambed line—a line from which the sense is carried on into
the next line. A short pause is necessary to indicate the end
of the line, *but no breath is taken*:

> The undiscover'd country from whose bourn //
> No traveller returns . . .
> > *Hamlet*

/

> The splendid silence clings //
> Around me: and around //
> The saddest of all kings,
> Crowned, and again discrowned.
>
> LIONEL JOHNSON, By the Statue of
King Charles at Charing Cross

We should also note the *Metrical Pause*, used to indicate the omission of a syllable or foot in a line of verse.

Verse and Prose Pauses

4. *The Rhetorical (or Sense) Pause*: Included in this category also is the breath pause. The student should not depend entirely upon the punctuation, which is not always infallible, for indication as to when to use this pause:

> Yes // they told me you were fools, // and that I was not to listen to your fine words // nor trust to your charity.
>
> BERNARD SHAW

5. *The Dramatic Pause :* This is a pause of emotion and is used to indicate intense feeling; it can be prolonged as long as the full power of the emotion can be sustained:

> Thou'lt come no more, //
> Never, never, never, never, never ! //
> Pray you, undo this button.
>
> King Lear

> That handkerchief which I so lov'd and gave thee
> Thou gav'st to // Cassio.
>
> Othello

6. *The Oratorical (or Emphatic) Pause :* A pause used to emphasize some particular word or phrase. This is especially useful in satiric verse and comedy :

> Sweep your own stable, trickster, //—married man.
>
> WILLIAM SHAKESPEARE

> Empty as death, Pervaneh, empty as // Death.
>
> JAMES ELROY FLECKER, Hassan

> And make the babbling gossip of the air
> Cry out, // "Olivia."
>
> *Twelfth Night*

Phrasing

Though phrasing was not included in our definition of modulation, it is so closely connected with pause that we shall do well to consider it here.

Phrasing is the dividing up of a sentence into groups of words, each group expressing one idea and of a length to be spoken in one breath. There is a short pause at the end of each phrase. The student must remember that phrasing depends on the *sense*. Therefore, when he breathes he must do so at the end of a phrase. On the one hand, he should not go on speaking until he has no more breath left; but, on the other, if the phrases are short he need not take in breath at the end of each one.

It should, for example, be possible to speak four lines of ten syllables each (pentameter) with one breath, though one rarely needs to do so.

Here is an example of a long phrase:

> ... And then, (*breath*)
> As night is withdrawn
> From these sweet-springing meads and bursting boughs of May,
> Dream ...
>
> ROBERT BRIDGES

and here an example of short phrasing:

> "Budge," says the fiend. "Budge not," says my conscience.
> "Conscience," say I, "you counsel well."
>
> *The Merchant of Venice*

We see, therefore, that we need phrasing both in order to make the sense of the passage clear, and also to allow us to take breath.

Phrasing is very important. In speaking prose or verse selections, the student, by dint of perseverance and suggestions from the teacher, usually, though not invariably, manages to phrase correctly, but the real test of good phrasing is in sight reading. There are surprisingly few students who can read aloud a moderately difficult passage of prose or verse and phrase it correctly the first time. This is due to the fact that they will not take the trouble to practise reading aloud and because they do not make good use of pause to give themselves time to look ahead. Where a breath is taken in the middle of a phrase the result is known as a *broken phrase*.

PRACTICAL EXERCISES

The reader will have gathered from the lesson that the very best exercise, both for pause and phrasing, is reading aloud.

Read prose and verse and vary your reading as much as possible— The Bible; Shakespeare; *The Times*; Milton; A. A. Milne; T. S. Eliot; Browning; Lamb; Bernard Shaw; Kipling; etc.

This type of exercise will not only improve your sight reading and enunciation, but will, at the same time, greatly increase your vocabulary and widen your knowledge of English literature. It will surprise you, too, how much better you will remember passages which you have read aloud.

EXERCISES IN THEORY

1. What is the importance of correct pause?
2. How many kinds of pause are there?
3. Name and give examples of the kinds of pause to be used in reading verse.
4. Name and give examples of the kinds of pause found in both prose and verse reading.
5. Which, do you think, might be the shortest pause, and which the longest?
6. A phrase is sometimes called a 'sense group.' Explain this.
7. Why is phrasing necessary?
8. What is a 'broken phrase'?
9. Select passages from well-known authors and phrase them.
10. Mark the phrases and name the pauses in Mark Antony's speech beginning:

Friends, Romans, countrymen . . .
Julius Cæsar, Act III, Scene 2

LESSON IX

INTERPRETATION AND
CHARACTERIZATION — GESTURE

THE subject of this lesson is a very important one for the would-be recitalist or actor. It is the point up to which all our preceding work has been leading. The foregoing lessons have dealt with the technique of speech, its scales and exercises, as it were. But perfect technique alone will never bring success —much less fame—to the performer, any more than a correctly played 'piece' will bring glory to the musician. Something more than that is needed; something unique and peculiar to the individual, which no teaching can give, but which springs from the soul of the performer and not from his mind—the spirit that 'maketh alive.'

In interpretation and characterization the performer should interweave his own individual conception and appreciation into that of the author. It is this 'original' element which is so often lacking in both young and old performers. As long as they have some one to imitate all goes well; but once they are asked to produce something of their own the result is lamentable.

It is possible, however, to err in the other direction. Some students, with originality and ideas, left to their own devices will produce a Hamlet or a Rosalind having no other con-nexion with the originals than the words they speak. The tendency of such performers, too, is to imagine that they can afford to dispense with technique. This is a great error. When the performer has become a famous actor he may, if he so desires, ignore details of technique, but woe to the student or beginner who does so!

There may be a well-known actress who constantly substitutes 'ter' for 'to.' The student who thinks he can do the same with impunity is heading for disaster.

Interpretation

Interpretation has two elements—something must be taken in before anything can be given out. The student must have understood and assimilated the author's meaning, mood, and feeling, and must then be able to present it in such a way that an audience can understand and appreciate them too. He must convey to his audience not only the facts, but the beauty of the passage— its word pictures and sound pictures, and the feeling or mood underlying them.

There are those who sacrifice sense to sound; others stress the meaning of a selection at the expense of its beauty. Let us keep to the middle path, avoiding both the deadly correctness of the 'technician' and the exaggerated 'feeling' of the sentimentalist.

Our first requirement is atmosphere. If we are interpreting a lyrical poem, for example, we must as far as possible enter into the thoughts and feelings of the poet when he wrote it. It is essential that we should know something of the poet, of his ideas and characteristics, and of the versification and metre of the poem; but these things must form the background for our atmosphere.

Let us take an example by way of illustration:

> There rose a hill that none but man could climb,
> Scarr'd with a hundred wintry water-courses—
> Storm at the top, and when we gain'd it, storm
> Round us and death.

In interpreting this passage it will help us to know that it is taken from Tennyson's *Holy Grail*—one of the *Idylls of the King*, a series of verse stories about Arthur and his knights. In this poem the Holy Vessel, which all the knights desired to see, was revealed to Sir Galahad—the purest of them all. The poem is written in blank verse, unrhymed lines of ten syllables with five stresses. This is our background.

But what we need to visualize is the word picture in these lines. No two people will imagine the same hill, and therein

lies the originality of interpretation. But we must *see* a hill—
its crest shrouded in dark clouds, pierced ever and anon by
blinding lightning flashes, which kindle the decayed, century-
old oaks; beneath the hill is the black, evil-smelling swamp,
spanned by the bridges along which Galahad sped. If we can
see in our minds that picture which the poet 'saw' as he wrote
we shall make it a living picture to our audience, but *not
otherwise*.

The student must be warned never to attempt a selection
which he does not fully understand. If he takes a passage
from a poem, then he must read through the whole poem to
be sure that he understands the relation of the particular
passage to the whole.

Characterization

Characterization is really interpretation applied to dramatic
work so that a character is correctly understood and rendered.
Here again, although the salient features of a character remain
always the same, there may be endless variety in their interpretation. That is why it is possible to witness a Shakespeare
play performed by a dozen different companies and to feel
each time that one has seen something new, because every
gifted actor will view the character he is portraying in a different
light, thus giving that 'infinite variety' which should be the
chief characteristic of his work.

Before beginning to study any particular character the
student should know something of the playwright. Then *the
whole play* must be read and digested, for any
'living' character must necessarily be influenced both by events and by the other
characters. In studying a character we need to
consider: first, what he does; second, what
he says; and third, what others say about him.
We should have a very incomplete idea of
Lear, or any other character, if we took into consideration his
own words only.

This point is equally important for those recitalists who take dramatic selections. It is not possible to determine the features of any character from one or two isolated speeches, nor should one be satisfied with vague ideas about the play as a whole. We must go to the source and study the play at first hand. Let us take, for instance, the character of Jacques in *As You Like It*. Who would fathom the embittered misanthropy of his speech on the seven ages of man if they had not followed his character from the beginning of the play and heard him talk with the Fool, with Orlando, and with the Duke's followers?

The famous "Quality of Mercy" speech, out of its context, might well be taken for the utterance of a sober sage, rather than that of a merry, loving woman disguised and enjoying it.

Gesture

In characterization, however, we have to consider something more than speech. Character is revealed as much by actions,

or gestures, as by speech itself. We shall deal with gestures more fully in the next lesson, but we may say in passing that

the kind of gesture used will depend largely on the period in which the action has been placed.

In the ancient Greek plays of Euripides (*Alcestis*) or

Sophocles (*Antigone*) the gesture was large, flowing, free, and beautiful. It was more or less stereotyped and was based

largely on the Greek frieze and offering movements, each gesture lasting as long as the emotion which dictated it.

The gesture of Elizabethan plays is still large, but more angular. It is influenced, too, by the dress of the period.

In the plays of Sheridan and Congreve gesture tended to become exaggerated and fussy—the fans of the ladies and the snuff-boxes of the men were not without their influence upon its characteristics.

Modern plays, on the other hand, show very little gesture at all compared with that of the earlier periods.

PRACTICAL EXERCISES

1. Take various lyrical poems, and, on the lines suggested in the lesson, work out what your approach to them would be. Then study and recite the poems. Vary your choice. Do not cling to one type of poem, merely because you like it or because you think it suits you.

   Here are a few suggestions:

   Blow, Blow, Thou Winter Wind (Shakespeare); *I Wandered Lonely as a Cloud* (Wordsworth); *Blest Pair of Sirens* (Milton); *Jim* (Hilaire Belloc); *Some One* (Walter de la Mare); *The Bailiff's Daughter of Islington*; *Frolic* (G. W. Russell).

2. Read aloud passages from plays which you know well (*A Midsummer Night's Dream*; *The Tempest*; *School for Scandal*; etc.); and then other passages from plays which you will need to read and study first (Ibsen; Shaw; D. Sayers; Barrie).

3. Read aloud some good one-act plays, paying close attention to characterization.

EXERCISES IN THEORY

1. What is meant by interpretation?

2. Is there any difference between interpretation and characterization?

3. Write brief notes on your method of approach to, and interpretation of, the following:

   The Donkey, G. K. Chesterton; *Allan-a-dale*; Psalm 23.

4. Write down what you consider to be the chief features of any four of the following characters:

   Hamlet; Touchstone (*As You Like It*); Viola (*Twelfth Night*); Tony Lumpkin (*She Stoops to Conquer*); Caliban (*The Tempest*); Joseph Surface (*School for Scandal*); Queen Elizabeth (*Will Shakespeare*).

5. How would you study a character?

6. In which order should you use the following: speech, thought, action?

7. Name the main types of gesture and briefly describe each.

GESTURE AND MIME

IT is very important that we should know quite definitely when and when not to use gesture. Generally speaking, gesture should not be employed in the reading or reciting of lyrical poems. Modulation of the voice and correct facial expression are usually all that are needed to interpret poems which deal chiefly with description, reflexion, and subjective emotion. Yet, even in these enlightened days, it is possible to meet teachers, especially of the very young, who insist on pointing to left and to right when these positions are named, and on holding up a hand to the ear to indicate listening.

> I listened, I opened,
> I looked to left and right.
> WALTER DE LA MARE

In the ballad, which has the form of the lyric but partakes of the character of the epic—since it deals with external events rather than feelings—it is permissible to indicate different speakers by a mere turn of the head, or character by a slight change of stance or posture, but a ballad must not be turned into a dramatic scene. The rhythmic flow of the ballad metre must be kept at all costs.

In prose selections, too, a little more freedom is allowed—a turn of the head to indicate different speakers, or pointing—though only where the passage absolutely demands it.

" 'In that direction,' said the Cat, waving its right paw round, ' lives a Hatter.' "

Gesture, properly speaking, belongs to drama, for drama means action. But even in dramatic work it is better to use too little gesture than too much; and infinitely better to use none at all, unless the gesture is spontaneous, springing from the emotions and adding something to the characterization.

To make movements merely for the sake of making them is disastrous; such movement will be lifeless, since it does not spring from the emotions, and it will inevitably detract from the character, for the attention of the audience will be drawn to any unnatural gesture.

Many promising students find this part of the work difficult, for they feel self-conscious and consequently their gesture is cramped and wooden. There are some, though not so many nowadays, who over-act. A quiet hour spent in studying Hamlet's advice to the Players, well-worn, but as true as ever, will not be wasted. We are not, by nature, a gesture-loving race and are too fond of 'bottling up' our emotions instead of letting them have free play.

The subject of gesture is much too extensive to be dealt with fully here, but we give a few suggestions which will help the student to work on right lines.

The root of much of the trouble is lack of relaxation. Some people never relax entirely, even when they are asleep. And that is why they get up feeling tired. All movement is made up of alternate tension and relaxation of the muscles. Children can readily be made to relax, if they are asked to pretend that they are rag dolls. Relaxation will be more complete if they first think they are wooden dolls—stiff in every part of the body.

The same exercises are equally useful for older students. It is a good plan, too, to lie flat on the floor, close your eyes, and try to imagine that you are sinking through the ground. In order to test relaxation, ask some one to lift a leg or an arm and let it drop.

When the student can relax at will he may begin to think about movement. Again, it is a good plan to think of all movement as springing from the centre of the body. It will then be co-ordinated and will cease to be the wooden, isolated reaction of one part.

Exercises for each part of the body—such as those given in the practical part of this lesson—should be practised, to music if possible. The student should take care to select good music

which will ensure that the movement is smooth and rhyth-
mical. These exercises will give ease and flexibility of movement, good stance and carriage.

Mime

Mime is dramatic action unaccompanied by words. Clearly,
therefore, the acting must be very good indeed if an idea or
emotion is to be conveyed to an audience solely through the
medium of gesture and facial expression.

For practical purposes we can divide mime into two categories :

1. *Occupational Mime*. This is concerned with actions in
imitation of real actions, such as sweeping, washing, laying a
table, dusting, posting a letter, etc. This type of mime is not
quite as easy as it sounds. The actor must, for example, be
careful not to walk through a table he has just dusted, nor
must he pick up a bucket from mid-air, or leave it there!

2. *Emotional Mime*. Here action is used, not to imitate real
action, but to display feelings of love, hate, despair, fear, anger,
joy, and so on.

It is well for the student to begin with occupational mime
and then to pass to the emotional. This is the easier way,
though it is possible to study and practise the two together.
Suitable material can be found in nursery rhymes, literary
characters, historical incidents—in fact in an almost limitless
and endlessly varied field.

In practising mime you should not use any gesture that is
cramped, slipshod, indefinite, or unnecessary. Remember that
all gesture has three parts—preparation, gesture proper, return.

PRACTICAL EXERCISES

A great part of this lesson must necessarily be devoted to exercises,
but time given to these will not be wasted.

Exercises for Different Parts of Body.

1. Feet (2:4 or 4:4 time)
   Stand with the feet about six inches apart as in the second
   position in Greek dancing.

Beginning with the right foot, raise the foot from heel to ball, and ball to toe tip, and back in the same way. Repeat four times with each foot.

2. Legs (2:4 or 4:4 time)

   (a) Stand with the feet in a small V. Raise the right knee, so that the foot just clears the floor. Swing the leg forward and back from the knee. Repeat four times with each leg. (Keeping the arms raised at shoulder level will help balance.)

   (b) Stand with the feet in small V. Swing the right leg as high as possible in front and behind. 1—forward; 2—together; 3—back; 4—together. Do not allow trunk to bend back and forward! Repeat four times with each leg.

3. *Trunk* (3:4 time—one bar for each movement)

   (a) Stand with the feet in the same position as for Exercise 2. Raise the arms, but not stiffly. 1—Swing trunk down; 2—Raise trunk and arms; 3—Stretch up on toes—hands pushing upward; 4—Lower to heels. Repeat four times.

(*b*) Stand with the feet again in the same position. Raise the arms to shoulder level and turn the trunk alternately to left and right. Repeat four times.

4. *Hands and Arms* (2:4 time)

   (*a*) Keep the arms at shoulder level but not stiff. Then lightly clench and open the hands. Repeat eight times.

   (*b*) Bend the hands up and down at the wrists. Then circle the hands at the wrists. Repeat each eight times.

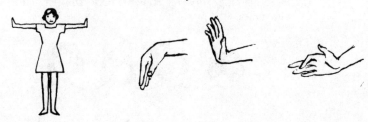

(c) (3:4 time). Bend the arms inward at the elbows with the palms facing the chest.

(d) Arm waving. Raise the arms to shoulder level; then draw the elbows in to the sides with the palms facing sideways. Push out the arms. The shoulder blades should be drawn together. Repeat eight times.

5. *Head* (3:4 time)
   (a) Head bending: forward; straight; back; straight. Repeat four times.

(b) Head bending: right; straight; left; straight. Repeat four times.

(c) Head turning: right; forward; left; forward. Repeat four times.

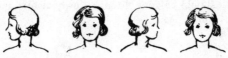

6. The Greek frieze movements may be used with advantage. Remember always to stand on the leg nearest the audience.

Exercises in Mime

1. Perform the actions of: dusting a room; gardening; knitting; scrubbing; washing; making-up.
2. Imagine that you are walking in various types of footwear or on different surfaces—in Wellingtons, high-heeled shoes, army boots, sandals; on concrete, in mud, in sand, over ploughed field, etc.
3. Act a characterization of different people—farm labourer, fashion model, old man, ballet dancer, paper boy, business man, soldier, Victorian, drunkard.
4. Represent in mime some *historical* or *literary character*— Queen Elizabeth, Lady Teazle, Rosalind, Tony Lumpkin, Joan of Arc, Julius Cæsar, Horatius, Mr Pickwick, Napoleon, Hitler, The Queen of Sheba.
5. If you can get others to work with you—and this is a good way to spend a winter's evening—plan scenes with an incident—a woman caught stealing, a street accident, a select party with an intoxicated 'gate crasher'—or scenes from history, etc.— the murder of Becket, Rebecca and Isaac, The Pied Piper, the murder of Rizzio, Alice in Wonderland, Winnie the Pooh, Robinson Crusoe.
6. (a) Imagine yourself some definite character sitting in a particular room. You hear a sound. You are doubtful

about it—it may be a burglar, or a fire alarm, or a welcome visitor. Represent all this in mime.

(b) Mime the following: You are cast on a desert island, exhausted and with all hope gone. You hear a noise; it is a plane; you make efforts to attract it; it comes down—or passes over.

7. Exercises for stage fall:

(a) Practise the series of movements shown in the pictures below, first to the right and then to the left. The actions should be gone through slowly at first and then gradually quickened.

(b) When you can fall easily to right or left practise backward and forward falls.

(c) Imagine that you are shot or stabbed, or receive bad news. Mime this, with the consequent collapse.

Remember always to give an upward lift to the body before falling.

EXERCISES IN THEORY

1. When should gesture be used?
2. What rules would you give to a student for the use of gesture.
3. How would you help a self-conscious student?
4. How would you help one whose tendency was to over-act?
5. What is mime?
6. Why is it advisable to practise to music? Why should one always use good music?
7. "Emotion should be expressed with every part of the body." How far do you agree with this?
8. Which do you consider to be more important, gesture or facial expression?

Give reasons for your answer.
9. Give in your own words the substance of Hamlet's advice to the players. (*Hamlet*, Act III, Scene 2.)

PROSODY — POETIC FORMS

PROSODY is not, as one might suppose, the study of prose, but is concerned with the science of versification—the different types of poetry, poetic form, metre, rhyme, and poetic licence. It comprises the rules for versification, but let us always bear in mind that it is 'poetry that makes the rules, not the rules poetry.' One cannot, by any stretch of the imagination, picture Milton sitting down with a book of rules for versification to write *Paradise Lost* or Shakespeare studying rules for drama when he wrote *A Midsummer Night's Dream.* Yet it is well for the student of elocution and literature to have an insight into these things and to learn to give them their proper place. They are scaffolding on which the building is erected, though not the building itself. Even genius may be fettered by rules. To what heights might not the great French dramatists, Corneille and Racine, have risen had they not been badgered by the rule-maniacs of their age! Let rules, then, have their proper place—and no more!

Types of Poetry

There are three main types of poetry—lyric, epic, and dramatic. Victor Hugo in his famous *Préface de Cromwell* said that the lyric was the poetry of the world's youth—hymns of praise to God; the epic, of its maturity—telling of the heroic deeds of the race; and the dramatic, of its old age— showing life with its intermingling of the sublime with the grotesque, tragedy with comedy.

Lyric Poetry (originally sung to the accompaniment of the lyre) is the poetry of thought, description, reverie, and sub- jective emotion. It describes feelings, not actions. A lyrical poem is usually written in stanzas and should be marked by continuity of thought. The different forms of lyric poetry will be dealt with later.

Epic, or *Heroic*, *Poetry* is grand and lofty in theme and style, recounting the deeds of gods and heroes—often demigods themselves—and great national events. It is usually written in continuous verse—*i.e.*, not divided into stanzas. One might describe it as gigantic, superhuman.

Some of the world's great epics are Homer's *Iliad* and *Odyssey*, Virgil's *Æneid*, Dante's *Divine Comedy*, Milton's *Paradise Lost*, the *Chanson de Roland*, and the *Niebelungenlied*.

It must not be imagined that every long poem is an epic. Such poems as *The Lady of the Lake* and *Marmion* are metrical romances, not epics.

 Dramatic Poetry is written in dialogue form and is intended to be acted. It is divided into three classes —tragedy, comedy, and history—though true drama may be said to contain both tragedy and comedy, providing contrast and relief for each other. Examples are seen in the Clown in *King Lear*, the Gravediggers in *Hamlet*, Juliet's nurse in *Romeo and Juliet*, Falstaff in *Henry IV*.

There are two other classifications of poetry which may be mentioned in passing—the *didactic*, which sets out to teach some moral lesson, and the *pastoral*, in which is rather formally portrayed the ideal simplicity of country life, with shepherds and shepherdesses as the main characters.

Poetic Form

Under this heading we may consider the different kinds of poem, chiefly lyrical—the ode, the elegy, the monody, the hymn, the sonnet, the ballad, and the French forms which have been introduced into English verse.

The Ode. In structure the ode is often based on the Greek choral ode, with strophe, antistrophe, and epode. It is usually long and complicated in construction, while the theme is lofty and the subject heroic, moral, or sacred. Examples of great

English odes are to be found in Keats's *Ode on a Grecian Urn*, Shelley's *Ode to the West Wind*, Milton's *Ode on the Morning of Christ's Nativity*, Wordsworth's *Ode to Duty* and *On Intimations of Immortality*.

The Elegy is a lyric devoted to mourning, expressing great grief. The usual elegiac metre is four lines of five iambs each (iambic pentameter), rhyming *abab* (Gray's *Elegy in a Country Churchyard*, Shelley's *Adonais*, Spenser's *Daphnaïda*, Byron's *Elegy on Newstead Abbey*).

The Monody is also a mourning song or poem, sung or spoken by a single mourner. An outstanding English example is Milton's *Lycidas*.

The Hymn—a sacred song or poem of thanksgiving, adoration, or praise, composed in a great variety of stanza forms and metres (*A Cradle Song*, by I. Watts, *A Christmas Hymn*, by A. Domett).

The Sonnet. This popular lyrical form is of Italian origin, and it has taken an important place in English verse. It must, therefore, be discussed a little more fully.

The sonnet, perfected by Dante and Petrarch in the thirteenth and fourteenth centuries, was introduced into England in the early sixteenth century by the poets the Earl of Surrey and Sir Thomas Wyatt. It is a poem of fourteen lines marked by unity of thought and divided into two parts—the octave (eight lines) and the sestet (six lines). Often the sonnet is arranged in two quatrains (stanzas of four lines) followed by two tercets (stanzas of three lines).

There are three main forms of the sonnet:

(a) *The Italian.* Here the rhymes are arranged *abba abba cde cde*. There is a definite break between the octave and the sestet; the rhymes of the sestet may be varied. Many of Milton's sonnets are on the Italian model—*e.g., Captain, or Colonel, or Knight in Arms*—as are also Drummond's sonnets and Rupert Brooke's *Clouds*.

(b) *The Modified Italian Sonnet.* Here the poets kept the traditional form, but made some alterations. For instance, they linked together the octave and the sestet as in Milton's *On his Blindness*.

(*c*) *The English Sonnet*. From the work of Spenser and Sidney the English Sonnet eventually emerged. This consists of three quatrains and a couplet. The rhyme scheme is *abab bcbc cdcd ee*. All Shakespeare's sonnets are of this pattern, except that his rhyme scheme is *abab cdcd efef gg*—e.g., *Shall I Compare Thee to a Summer's Day?*

The Ballad. The ballad, though lyrical in form, partakes, in a small degree, of the character of the epic, in that it deals, not with thoughts and feelings, but with external events, usually love or war. It is written usually in four-lined stanzas rhyming *abab*.

> Ben Battle was a soldier bold,
> And used to war's alarms;
> But a cannon-ball took off his legs,
> So he laid down his arms!

The older ballads tell a simple story without comment of any kind.

Examples of ballads are: *Lord Ullin's Daughter*, *Allan-a-dale*, *The Wife of Usher's Well*.

Certain verse-forms for light-hearted lyrics have been imported into English literature from the French. The best known are the Ballade, the Chant Royal, the Rondeau, the Rondel, and Villanelle, and the Triolet.

The Ballade. This is a poem of three stanzas, each of seven, eight, or ten lines, with an envoy of four or five lines. The rhyme scheme for the eight-line stanza is *ababbcbc* (three rhymes only) and of the envoy *bcbc*. (An example is provided by *A Ballade to Queen Elizabeth*—A. Dobson.)

The Chant Royal is really a longer form of the ballade. It has five stanzas of eleven lines each, and an envoy of five lines.

The Rondeau consists of thirteen eight-syllable lines with two rhymes. The first line is used as a refrain at the end of the second and third stanza. (*In Rotten Row*—Henley.)

The Rondel is a variation of the rondeau.

The Villannelle has five stanzas of three lines each and one of four lines, lines 1 and 3 being repeated as refrain in lines 6, 12, 18, and 9, 15, 19, respectively. The rhyme scheme is *aba* (for three stanzas), *abaa* (for the fifth).

The Triolet is a poem of eight lines. The first line is repeated in the fourth and seventh, and the second in the eighth. The rhyme scheme is *abaaabab*. (*When First We Met*, by Robert Bridges.)

Clearly there can be no great depth of thought in poems of this type, for the complicated rhyme scheme and refrain arrangement must necessarily tend to give them a superficial and artificial character.

PRACTICAL EXERCISES

1. Find examples of the forms given in the lesson.
   Mark down the rhyme scheme and number of syllables.
2. Read passages from good translations of the *Iliad* and *Æneid*.

EXERCISES IN THEORY

1. What is meant by prosody?
2. Into what 'types' would you divide poetry?
   Give examples of each.
3. What are the main differences between lyric and epic poetry?
4. Name the different kinds of drama.
5. Name the different poetic forms.
6. Describe the sonnet form, giving examples of each type.
7. Name and describe the French metrical forms.
8. In what way does the ballad differ from other lyrical forms?

PROSODY—RHYTHM, METRE, RHYME, ETC.

WE must distinguish carefully between rhythm and metre, for, though they are closely related, they are not the same. It is possible to have rhythm in prose, but metre belongs to verse only.

Rhythm

Rhythm has been defined in hundreds of different ways, which goes to show how difficult it is to define. It is the measured flow which we find in music and verse and in

movements such as dancing, machinery, and the waves of the sea. In verse it is heard in the recurrence of stressed syllables at comparatively regular intervals. It is also to be seen in dancing. Some claim that the balance and harmony to be seen in painting and sculpture are also a form of rhythm and they are certainly closely related.

Metre

The flow of rhythm in verse follows a variety of patterns or measures, depending upon the distribution of stressed and unstressed syllables. Thus we get a regular beat to a line of poetry:

> So àll dày lòng the nòise of bàttle ròlled
> or : And his còhòrts were gleàming with pùrple and gòld,

This regularity of measure in verse is known as the metre, and is divided into feet, with, as a rule, one stressed syllable to each foot. So, for the verses above, we have:

$$. \ \setminus | . \ \setminus | . \ \setminus | . \ \setminus | . \ \setminus | \quad — \text{ five feet, each} . \ \setminus$$
$$\text{and:} .. \ \setminus | .. \ \setminus | .. \ \setminus | .. \ \setminus | \quad — \text{ four feet, each} .. \ \setminus$$

According to the number of feet to a line of verse it is called: monometer (one foot); dimeter (two); trimeter (three); tetrameter (four); pentameter (five); hexameter (six); septameter (seven); octameter (eight).

Poems are usually divided into groups of lines, each group following the same pattern of length of line and rhyming scheme. Such a group is known as a *stanza*. A stanza must not be called a 'verse,' for 'a verse' is a single line of poetry, whereas 'verse' is used in reference to poetry as a whole. A stanza may consist of any number of lines from two upwards.

A two-line stanza forms a couplet, or distich; a three-line, a tercet (or triplet, if all lines rhyme); a four-line, a quatrain; a five-line, a quintain; a six-line, a sestet (or sextain); a seven-line, a heptastich (or, when arranged in a certain way, a Rhyme Royal); an eight-line, ottava-rima. Nine lines have been used in the Spenserian Stanza, while Dante in his *Divine Comedia* employed a stanza of thirteen lines (terza rima).

English verse has four main metres.

1. *Iambic* (or *double rising*): two syllables in each foot—an unstressed followed by a stressed, *e.g.*, abùse.

> I càn | nót sèe | whàt flòwers | àre àt | mỳ feèt. |
> KEATS

This is a line of five iambs and is, therefore, called an iambic pentameter.

2. *Trochaic* (or *double falling*): two syllables in each foot—a stressed followed by an unstressed, *e.g.*, hàrpèr.

> Tàste nót | whèn thè | wìne-cùp | glìstèns.

This is a line of four trochees, called a trochaic tetrameter.

3. *Anapæstic* (or *treble-rising*): three syllables in a foot—two unstressed followed by a stressed, *e.g.*, disàppèar.

> Fòr thè Àng | èl òf Deàth | sprèad his wìngs | òn thè blàst.
> BYRON

This is an anapæstic tetrameter.

4. *Dactylic* (or *treble-falling*): three syllables to the foot—one stressed followed by two unstressed, *e.g.*, hàppily.

Brìghtèst aǹd | bèst òf tʰe | sons òf tʰe | mòrning

—a dactylic tetrameter.

There are one or two other metrical feet to be noticed; it will be seen that they are irregular in that they do not follow the usual rule of one stressed syllable to a foot:

Spondee—two stressed syllables : àmèn.

Choriamb—four syllables, a trochee + an iamb.

Pyrrhic—two unstressed syllables : of a.

Tribrach—three unstressed syllables.

The following rhyme will help the student to memorize these metres:

Trochee trips from long to short;
From long to long in solemn sort
Slow *Spondee* stalks; strong foot! yet ill able
Ever to come up with *Dactyl* trisyllable.
Iambics march from short to long;—
With a leap and a bound the swift Anapæsts throng.

COLERIDGE

It is well to avoid speaking of 'long' and 'short' syllables in English verse. These terms properly apply to classical verse, which depends upon quantity and not upon stress.

Rhyme

Rhyme is not essential to English poetry. Much of our greatest poetry, by such poets as Milton, Shakespeare, and Tennyson, has been written in blank verse, which is unrhymed. We have already seen that excessive repetition of rhyme and complicated metre leads to light, frivolous verse. Usually the loftier the verse, the simpler the form, because the poet needs to be freed from the constraint of rules.

Rhyme is the correspondence of sounds usually to be found at the ends of lines of poetry. Such rhymes as 'bull' and 'pull' are known as masculine, whereas double rhymes like 'patter' and 'hatter' are feminine.

Three-syllabled rhyme is usually only found in humorous verse, though Thomas Hood's *Bridge of Sighs* is an exception to this.

Alliteration is the repetition of consonantal sound and is sometimes called *head rhyme*.

> I murmur under moon and stars.

> I bubble into eddying bays,
>   I babble on the pebbles.
>   TENNYSON, *The Brook*

Assonance is the repetition of the vowel sound.
    e.g., dole; cope.

Rhyme Scheme. In noting the rhyme scheme of a poem letters of the alphabet are used—thus:

Come away, come away, death,	*a*
And in sad cypress let me be laid;	*b*
Fly away, fly away, breath.	*a*
I am slain by a fair cruel maid.	*b*
My shroud of white, stuck all with yew,	*c*
O! prepare it!	*d* (feminine)
My part of death no one so true	*c*
Did share it	*d*

Twelfth Night

Heroic Couplet. Lines of five iambs rhyming *aabbcc* are known as heroic couplets. If the sense ends with the lines, they are called closed couplets.

> So peaceful rests, without a stone, a name,
> What once had beauty, titles, wealth and fame.
> ALEXANDER POPE,
> *Elegy to the Memory of an Unfortunate Lady*

Those who would try to write poetry must avoid:
1. Hackneyed rhymes (love, dove).
2. Repeated rhymes (pressed, repressed; nation, carnation).
3. Cockney rhymes (dawn, corn; paw, door).

The 'eye rhyme,' however, when words are similar in spelling but not in sound (rough, bough), is sometimes allowed.

The work of even the greatest poet would become very monotonous if he kept rigidly to the rules of versification. It is often the variations that make verse interesting and beautiful. Thus it is that certain 'licences,' or allowable variations, have come to be recognized. They may be divided into three classes: Licence in spelling, in grammar, and in metre.

1. *Spelling.* Under this we may class:

    (*a*) *Elision.* The omission of a letter or syllable.

        when'er; th'universe; 'tis

Milton uses elision very frequently—*e.g.*:

> Temper'd to th'oaten flute.

    (*b*) *Prothesis.* The addition of a word or syllable.

        yclad; beteem.

2. *Grammar.*

    Ellipsis. The omission of words that are not absolutely necessary to the sense.

        'Here!' for 'Come here.'

3. *Metrical.*

    (*a*) *Inversion.* Replacing one metrical foot by another —*i.e.* Iamb for trochee: anapaest for dactyl, and *vice versa.*

> And did those feet in ancient time
> Walk upon England's mountains green.

(b) *Substitution.* An anapaest replaced by an iamb, or a dactyl by a trochee.

(c) *Hypermetric Foot* (Feminine ending)—the addition of a syllable at the end of a line.

> To be or not to be, that is the question.

(d) *Anacrusis.* The addition of a syllable at the beginning of a line.

> *But* Hail, thou goddess sage and holy

(e) *Catalectic Foot.* The omission of a syllable at the end of a line:

> Brightest and best of the sons of the morning.

(f) *Initial Truncation.* A syllable cut off at the beginning of the line.

> Tread softly, because you tread on my dreams.

When you are scanning it is advisable to mark the stressed syllables throughout the passage or stanza. However irregular the verse, some line or part of it is sure to reveal the original metre.

In the study of a poem, all these points must be noted, but not to the extent of excluding all else. Too much analysis will destroy the beauty of any poem. We need, too, to see how the poet makes the sound fit the sense; what use he makes of alliteration, assonance, and onomatopœia; whether long or short vowels predominate; and, finally, whether he uses figures of speech, and if so, which ones.

Poets will be found to make frequent use of onomatopœia, particularly in descriptive passages. This is a device in which a word is formed to imitate a sound—*e.g., pop, plop, cuckoo, hum, buzz*—

> Whistle of bombs and blast and crash,
> Ear-splitting smash
> Of unnumbered panes of glass.
> J. G. M.

> Bells, bells, bells—
> From the gingling and the tinkling of the bells.
> E. A. POE

Figures of Speech

The figures of speech most commonly used are: the simile, the metaphor, personification, antithesis, and apostrophe.

Simile. The introduction of a comparison to make a description more vivid.

> The Assyrian came down *like a wolf on the fold.*

Metaphor. The replacing of one thing by another which resembles it in some way.

> All the world's a stage.

Personification. The giving of life to lifeless objects.

> Blind with thine hair the eyes of Day.
>
> Laughter holding both his sides.

Antithesis. The setting of words in contrast to one another. It is possible to have:

Single Antithesis:	Light after darkness.
Double Antithesis:	*To err* is human: *to forgive* divine.
Triple Antithesis:	If a *tyrant* can *conquer* with *slaves,* what may not a *just ruler accomplish* with *the free.*
Implied Antithesis:	His form and cause conjoined, *preaching to stones.*
	Would make them capable.
	(What, then, would it not do to men!

Apostrophe. The addressing of direct speech to some quality as though to a person, or to the absent as if they were present.

> Frailty, thy name is woman!

EXERCISES IN THEORY

1. Take a good anthology of verse and scan stanzas from different poems, noting metre, rhyme scheme, and any examples of poetic licence.
2. What do you consider to be the difference between rhythm and metre?
3. What are the four main metres? Give examples.

4. Name and give examples of the different types of stanza.
5. What is (a) rhyme, (b) alliteration, (c) assonance? Give examples of each.
6. Explain and give examples of: (a) elision, (b) ellipsis, (c) prothesis.
7. What is a figure of speech? · Name four and give one example of each.
8. If you were asked to point out the aesthetic qualities of a poem, for what would you look?
9. Try to find other examples of the four types of antithesis.
10. Write an appreciation of any two of the following poems and say how you would interpret them.

Bridges: *Nightingales*
Keats: *To Autumn*
Browning: *The Last Ride Together*

LESSON XIII

SPEAKING IN PUBLIC

It falls to comparatively few of us to appear on the concert platform or on the stage, but there are very few who, at some time or another, are not called upon to make a speech. True, it may be only to open a bazaar, or garden party, or to propose a vote of thanks, but, nevertheless, it is a prospect which fills most of us with dread. Even seasoned actors have been known to lose their nerve when they have to stand up and give voice to their own ideas, instead of interpreting some one else's.

Now, while it is an excellent thing to be able to recite a poem or portray a character in a play, if we cannot give voice to our own thoughts and ideas we are rather like a painter who can only copy some other artist's work.

Let us then consider how we can learn to speak easily and fluently in public.

Clearly the first essential is to have something to say. That seems obvious enough, yet how often we hear speakers who drone on endlessly and at the end have said nothing at all! We must have ideas, and we must have a reasonably good vocabulary with which to express them. It is an awful thing to be 'stuck' for a word, and most of us, including those who have had the benefit of a grammar-school or public-school education, have a very limited vocabulary.

The best way to improve one's vocabulary and English generally is by reading good books—'ancient' or modern—with an equally good dictionary at hand. It does not help to know a word if one is not sure of pronunciation or meaning. There are plenty of Mrs Malaprops in the world (only recently we were informed that a motion had been passed 'magnanimously'). Then one should listen to *good* speakers on radio and television; but again we must stress the *good*, for one hears far too many mistakes from television orators—such as 'different to' (instead of from), split infinitives ('to always go'), and bad speech ('idea*r* of,' 'I saw(r) a'); and how many of them trot out weird Americanized pronunciations—prim*a*rily, 'subs*i*dence.' So listen critically, and check by your Oxford Dictionary (or Webster's). Your dictionary must be your constant companion.

A good rule to remember is that one should never use a long word where a short one will do. I remember a great speaker once saying, "It is not written, 'In the commencement God made heaven and earth,' but 'in the *beginning*.'" How people love to 'commence' everything! Nor should a speaker use long, involved sentences in which he himself often loses the thread—to say nothing of the unfortunate listeners! Sainte-Beuve's rule, "one sentence, one idea" is a good one to follow.

Wide reading, in addition to increasing our vocabulary, will help to increase our knowledge, our stock of ideas, and will provide us, too, with useful quotations and references.

We shall need much practice before we are ready to speak fluently in public. It is wise, at first, to do this practice in the privacy of one's own room, preferably before a large mirror. We have already learned how to stand in an easy, relaxed position: firmly planted, shoulders braced, but not stiff, chin level, eyes forward. From the beginning watch yourself critically. Many speakers sway to and fro as they speak, until the audience becomes almost seasick, others develop exaggerated and distracting gestures, and I can think of one of our great politicians who has an irritating habit of repeating the same meaningless circular movement of the hand.

Having taken up your position, begin by telling your invisible audience a simple story. Choose, if you like, a fairy-tale where you are sure of the facts. Tell it simply, and as dramatically as you can. It is a good plan to imagine you have an audience of children. Use simple 'language' and speak slowly: when you need to pause for breath—or an idea—do not say *um* or *er* (this is a bad habit). There is nothing against a second's pause—indeed, it can often be used to great effect. Remember that when you speak in a large hall you must throw your voice to the back row: there is no need to shout if the voice is well forward and resonant.

From simple children's stories go on to Biblical or historical ones. Wherever possible, make your story interesting by using direct speech. To say, "He said he would kill her if she did that again," is much less exciting than, "He said, 'I'll *kill* you if you ever do that again.'"

When you feel that you have become a proficient story-teller, try yourself out on a 'live' audience. Try it on the children, on younger brothers and sisters. You will never have a more critical audience, because as soon as they are bored they will get up and walk away, leaving you high and dry, which grown-up audiences unfortunately cannot do.

When you have mastered this stage it is a good plan to speak for three or four minutes on a variety of subjects—descriptions of places, hobbies, current events, world problems. Again it is a help if you can get some knowledgeable person to listen and criticize, or, if you have access to a tape recorder, listen to yourself as your own critic, ready to condemn mercilessly dullness, mumbling, hesitancy, and 'woolly' wandering.

The old rule, 'Stand up, speak up, and shut up' has something to be said for it. When you are speaking in public say clearly and distinctly what you have to say, and then stop. Never imagine that you will be criticized for brevity, for the best speaker in the world cannot hold attention beyond a certain time. Far more people would go to church if they could be sure that the sermon would not last more than fifteen minutes. Naturally, if you are asked to deliver an hour's lecture on some subject or other, then an hour's lecture it must be. It is essential to know your facts and to plan your talk carefully under headings. Every speech, however long or short, should have three parts: (*a*) the introduction; (*b*) the main, 'meaty' part; and (*c*) the conclusion.

Unless you are very sure of yourself and of your subject matter you will need notes. These should be clearly written and large enough to see easily without having to peer down constantly. Many speakers like to put each note on a separate small sheet, but remember this can be disastrous if you drop them, or they blow away. The main thing is that you should be able to refer to them, without constant pauses, which break up the continuity of thought.

Bazaar opening, votes of thanks, and opening remarks should be short and clear. Sometimes it happens that the Chairman's 'opening remarks' are longer than the main speech. One should, if possible, try to vary or avoid the routine openings— "It gives me great pleasure," "It is my privilege," etc.

Some speakers begin by saying, "I really do not know why I have been asked to come here" or "I do not know anything about this subject," and then speak for about half an hour to prove that they do. Avoid all such trite remarks.

Funny stories, though they sometimes enliven a dull evening, should be avoided, unless they spring naturally from the context of the speech. Sometimes, when the audience is hostile or unresponsive, an amusing and apt story introduced at the beginning will 'break the ice' and cause them to listen more sympathetically. Never talk down to your audience, and never belittle them; this will certainly 'rub them up the wrong way.' Indeed, it is a wise plan to flatter audiences a little by stressing your own unworthiness. Do not talk above their heads, or they will be bored, will cough and fidget (a sure sign of lack of interest).

It is not wise to ask rhetorical questions—*i.e.*, ones to which the speaker expects no answer. You may have a joker in the audience, and it is a little disconcerting when one asks, "Who would be so foolish as to venture on such a course?" to have some one shout back, "You would, Gov'nor!"

To sum up, speakers must be audible, and should endeavour to be entertaining as well as instructive—above all, they must be brief and businesslike. As in all other work, modulation is very important. Change pitch and pace if you want to keep your audience awake, and when they are dropping off introduce a sudden pause.

If you have to speak into a microphone do not stand too close or bawl into it, and do not turn your head from side to side, or move backward and forward, so that the volume of sound is changed. Speak clearly (paying attention to consonants at the end of words) and not too fast. This does not mean that the rate of speech should not be varied: a quick phrase can be very 'telling,' but pauses must *never* be left out.

Finally, remember that good speech needs practice. Think of Demosthenes, who is said to have practised on the seashore, speaking over the noise of the waves, with pebbles in his mouth and a dagger suspended over his shoulder, so that he should be pricked every time he raised it. If public speakers all dealt with their failings as firmly there would be fewer boring speakers.

Deal equally harshly with your own failings, and people will then listen to you gladly. Cease to be self-critical, and you will become the deadly bore, whom suffering and captive audiences would gladly murder. Above all, speak with conviction. An audience cannot be expected to accept what you say if you speak in a half-hearted manner. There is no need to thump the table (or the Bible) to give added force to your speech. If you believe what you say, your voice and manner must show it, and if you don't believe it, it is better unsaid.

PRACTICAL EXERCISES

1. Tell the story of either (*a*) The Three Bears, (*b*) Red Riding Hood, or (*c*) Cinderella to an imaginary audience of children.
2. You have before you a group of teenagers. Tell the story of (*a*) Moses, (*b*) Joseph, (*c*) The Nativity.
3. Describe to an adult audience (*a*) a famous place you have visited, (*b*) your hobby, (*c*) the most exciting event in your life.
4. Read an article from a good newspaper; reproduce it in your own words.
5. Propose a vote of thanks to a lecturer at a scientific (or any society) meeting.
6. Imagine that you are invited to open the Church Fête or Bazaar.
7. You are at an Old Boys' (or an Old Girls') Dinner. You are asked to propose the toast to the School.
8. Imagine that you are Chairman at a meeting at which some important personality is to speak. Give your opening remarks and introduce the speaker.

SPEAKING TOGETHER

For years now the old-fashioned class recitation has definitely been 'out.' And rightly so, if by class recitation is meant the singsong drone practised by a bored class of children, under the direction of an equally bored teacher. But I, for one, can recall to-day poems taught me in my early years by an enlightened and enthusiastic teacher (though no specialist in Speech Training), which we all enjoyed reciting together, and which, even by specialist standards, were well spoken.

Choral Speaking, or speaking together, can be a joy to young and old, and in schools or teachers' training colleges it could be developed with advantage. Firstly, it provides a means of improving standards in speech where individual lessons are not possible. Working together, in speech as in all else, encourages team spirit, and, in addition, the nervous, shy individual, who is afraid to open his mouth, gains confidence from the group, while the overconfident one learns restraint.

Moreover, not only is speech itself improved, but Choral Speaking can be used to teach appreciation of language and verse, and to develop a sense of rhythm and speech value. And while this can be tackled in the classroom with large groups of quite small children, it can also lead, with adult choirs, to advanced and skilful performance of a very high quality.

From earliest times people have found joy in speaking and singing together, and very often the chant—as in the Greek chorus and the chants of primitive peoples—came nearer to speech than to song. Such was the case, too, in the Psalms of the Hebrews, their balanced verses being spoken by different groups of people.

The operative word in Choral Speaking is uniformity, or—horrible term—togetherness. Let us take a group of complete beginners. We must, of course, begin with uniformity of sounds and these (see Lessons I and II) can be practised together, but we must not wait for perfection before moving on to the next stage, or our class will be bored at the outset.

It is a good plan to start the class each time with a short practice of vowels and consonants. If after a few lessons we discover a marked 'delinquent,' a little individual help will usually put the matter right.

Now for our group. The ideal number lies between fifteen and twenty-five, but we cannot, of course, always have the size of group we want, and it is possible to work with larger groups, but preferably not more than twenty-five. Indeed, I have heard very effective speaking from a group of over one hundred, though this is not to be recommended, since it requires a highly skilled teacher and a very well-trained group. It is first of all essential that all members should be able to see the teacher-conductor.

We can arrange our group thus:

```
O    o    o    o    o    o    o
   o    o    o    o    o    o
      o    o    o    o    o
```

or some teachers prefer to have a double semicircle:

```
              x    x    x
          x      x    x     x
       x    x              x    x
     x    x                  x
   x    x          X          x
```

The group must first learn to follow the directions of the teacher-conductor. No exaggerated movements are required for this. A simple movement of the hand to mark the 'beat' of the verse, moving from left to right on one line and back on the next. The other hand will be used to indicate increase (or decrease) of volume. Later on, the choir will learn to dispense with a conductor completely.

We shall, first of all, take simple nursery rhymes and jingles. Attack (starting together) is very important—*and* difficult. It is a good idea to encourage the group to breathe in lightly as the conductor's hand is raised and to speak the first word as it drops (this is a great help later on when they must start alone). However simple the work, if singsong monotony is to be avoided great attention must go to modulation (Lessons VI–VIII), pitch and pace and volume must be changed according to the sense and pauses stressed, though *not* to the detriment of the rhythm.

Once this preliminary work has been mastered, it is possible to pass on to simple poems. There are, to-day, some excellent collections of poems suitable for Choral Speaking. There is certainly no lack of material, but in the early stages the teacher should choose simple poems (this does not mean childish ones, but such as tell a simple story or express simple, clear thought) and poems which have a definite rhythm. Ballads and short narrative poems are excellent.

If a poem is to be spoken intelligently, whether by an individual or a group, *it must* be understood. So it is a good plan to devote a few minutes to discussing the poem, its general meaning, its mood and content, and how this is to be interpreted. The teacher-conductor should invite suggestions even from the youngest, so that *all* feel they have an interest in the work in hand. Once every one is agreed on the interpretation the work can go forward.

Monotony, flatness, pedestrian rhythm are the snares that beset the new choir, so that it cannot be stressed too often that in order to avoid monotony, pitch, pace, and volume must be changed according to the sense of the passage. Perhaps change of pace or rate is the most difficult for a choir, who will either drawl—each one waiting for his neighbour—or gabble, so that clarity is lost.

It is therefore advisable, from time to time, to choose poems which will illustrate different paces. *E.g.*, "Slow horses, slow, as through the woods we go," for slow pace, and R. L. Stevenson's *From a Railway Carriage* for practice in rapid speaking,

while the dance of Pau-Puk-Keewis from *Hiawatha* is admirably
suited to show the transition from slow pace, through medium,
to fast.

> First he danced a solemn measure,
> Very slow in step and gesture,
> In and out among the pine-trees,
> Through the shadows and the sunshine,
> Treading softly like a panther.
> Then more swiftly and still swifter,
> Whirling, spinning round in circles,
> Leaping o'er the guests assembled,
> Eddying round and round the wigwam,
> Till the leaves went whirling with him,
> Till the dust and wind together
> Swept in eddies round about him.
>
> LONGFELLOW, *Hiawatha's Wedding-feast*

Change of volume, too, is equally important, and teachers will
have no difficulty in finding selections where one stanza, line,
or phrase needs to be spoken softly, and another loudly (as in
Tennyson's "Blow, bugle, blow").

It is a good plan to introduce solo speakers from time to time,
but the teacher should not make the mistake of giving solo parts
to the same people every time, because they speak well. For a
public performance obviously one must choose the best, but in
private practice the quietest mouse is the one who will benefit
most from the chance to speak a line alone. In *Lord Ullin's
Daughter*, for instance, different speakers can say the words of
the chieftain, the boatman, the father, and the daughter. Then
there are poems, including many of Shakespeare's lyrics, where
a soloist or a small group can speak the stanza and the choir
join in the refrain.

> SOLO. It was a lover and his lass,
> CHOIR. With a hey, and a ho, and a hey nonino.
> SOLO. That o'er the green cornfield did pass,
> CHOIR. In the spring time, the only pretty ring time,
> When birds do sing, hey ding a ding, ding;
> Sweet lovers love the spring.

Our next step, with an older choir, will be to divide the group according to voices—A for high and B for low (or, if we have a mixed adult choir, it is possible to have four groups).

```
A    A    A    A    B    B    B
   A    A    A    B    B    B
     A    A    B    B    B
```

With such an arrangement the A's can speak one stanza (or part of it) and the B's the other. This is especially suitable for the Psalms, which, as we have said, were originally spoken in this way.

PSALM 24   A. Who is this King of glory?
            B. The Lord strong and mighty, etc.
(or) PSALM 23 A. He maketh me to lie down in green pastures,
            B. He leadeth me beside the still waters.
            A and B. He restoreth my soul.

Further variety can be introduced by speaking in sequence, as for instance in Christina Rossetti's *Goblin Market*. The whole choir may speak the first lines, and then individuals in turn repeat the list of fruits:

UNISON.   Morning and evening
               Maids heard the goblins cry:
GROUP A.   Come buy our orchard fruits,
               Come buy, come buy:
        1. Apples and quinces,
        2. Lemons and oranges,
        3. Plump unpecked cherries,
        4. Melons and raspberries,
        5. Bloom-down-checked peaches,
        6. Swart-headed mulberries,
        7. Wild free-born cranberries,
        8. Crab-apples, dewberries,
        9. Pine-apples, blackberries,
       10. Apricots, strawberries;—

UNISON.	All ripe together.
	In summer weather,—
	Morns that pass by,
	Fair eves that fly;
	Come buy, come buy:
CUMULATIVE 1.	Our grapes fresh from the vine,
+ 2.	Pomegranates full and fine.
+ 3.	Dates and sharp bullaces,
+ 4.	Rare pears and greengages,
+ 5.	Damsons and bilberries,
ALL.	Taste them and try:
+ 6.	Currants and gooseberries,
+ 7.	Bright fire-like barberries,
+ 8.	Figs to fill your mouth,
+ 9.	Citrons from the South,
ALL.	Sweet to tongue and sound to eye;
	Come buy, come buy.

.   .   .   .

The Keys of the Kingdom may also be treated in this way, or if preferred may be used for cumulative speaking, one member or small group joining in on each new line.

The Twelve Days of Christmas is another good selection for cumulative speaking, and many others are to be found in good anthologies.

Later on the advanced choir may try experiments in descants. This is difficult and needs much practice in separate groups. A passage spoken in monotone by one group as a bass and the inflected speech of the remainder can be very effective.

Many such experiments may be tried out, once the basic work is there, but it is unwise to embark on any such ambitious venture until the choir or group is thoroughly drilled in all the preliminary work. We must, like all good craftsmen, first master the secrets of our mystery, and never lose sight of the fact that we are the humble interpreters of a poet's thoughts and feelings.

IN CONCLUSION

WE have sought in the foregoing lessons to give the student an outline of his subject. We would not for one moment have him think that the last word has been said on this extensive theme, but maybe the taste he has been given will encourage him to drink deeper.

There is so much more that might be said about the speaking of different kinds of verse, and about choral verse-speaking, which as yet is in its infancy and with which so much might be done, especially in our schools.

Nor would we conclude without a last word of warning to the student. Let your aim ever be beauty, truth, and sincerity, and not adherence to rules. How much harm has been done, how much promising work spoilt by the mania for classification, rules, and regulation! Let them be your servants, not your master.

Use moderation in all things. And finally . . . " Whatsoever things are true; whatsoever things are lovely; whatsoever things are of good report, think on *these* things."